stan

D1613139

The Account Books of

BENJAMIN MILDMAY, EARL FITZWALTER

THE AUTHOR

A. C. Edwards is a Somerset man who has spent two-thirds of his life in Essex. He read history at the University of Bristol and taught at Arnold School, Blackpool, and Maldon Grammar School. In 1949, he became history adviser to the Essex Education Department and lecturer to the Essex Record Office. At the Record Office, his brief was to make the original evidence of local history known by lecturing and writing about it and by arranging and running exhibitions, chiefly at Ingatestone Hall. This was then a unique post, but over the years a number of museums and record offices have made similar appointments.

His writings include *English History from Essex Sources*, 1550-1750, *A History of Essex*, *Royalty in Essex*, and a number of the well-known picture books published by the Essex Record Office.

He retired in 1968, but still keeps busy. His book, *John Petre*, a closely-knit collection of essays on the first Lord Petre, was published by the Regency Press in December 1975. His main hobby is examining the structure of ancient timber-framed buildings in order to determine their dating and development. His only ambition has been to write just one book of really superb quality. He likes most people but prefers cats.

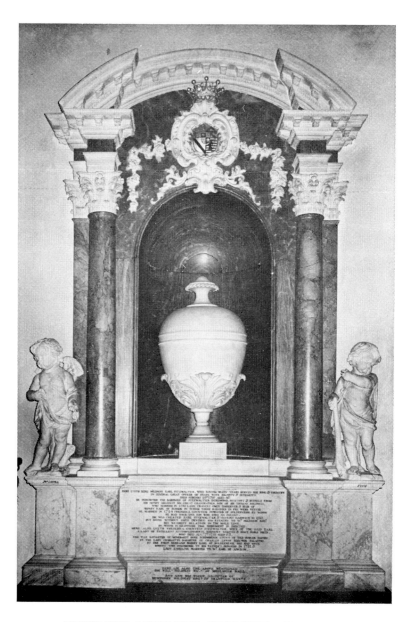

FITZWALTER MONUMENT, CHELMSFORD CATHEDRAL

The Account Books of

BENJAMIN MILDMAY, EARL FITZWALTER

by

A. C. EDWARDS

REGENCY PRESS
LONDON AND NEW YORK

*

23554

942·67 ED

© Copyright. A. C. EDWARDS, 1977

This book is copyrighted under the Berne Convention.
No portion may be reproduced by any process without
the copyright holder's written permission except for the
purposes of reviewing or criticism, as permitted under
the Copyright Act of 1956.

Made and printed in Great Britain for
REGENCY PRESS (London and New York) LTD.
43 NEW OXFORD STREET, LONDON, WC1A 1BH

CONTENTS

ILLUSTRATIONS

ACKNOWLEDGMENTS

If it had not been for the kindness of my friend and former colleague, K. C. Newton, the Essex County Archivist, this book would not have been published. It was originally intended to be one of a new series of edited local texts which he had planned, but when its preparation was almost completed, the economic blizzard struck the series and, indeed, most of the publishing activities of the Essex Record Office. Then, the Regency Press became interested in Essex local history; it published my *John Petre*, and, with its close colleagues, Witham Printing Ltd., offered to take over this Fitzwalter book. Ken Newton immediately and generously encouraged me to accept, and he has since read the proofs and made helpful suggestions.

Another friend and former colleague, Nancy Briggs, Supervisor of the Students' Room at the Essex Record Office, has also very kindly read the proofs and made many useful comments.

I have been unable to get in touch with Valerie Cooper. As a sixth former she produced two admirable essays on the origins of the Mildmay family; these have been very helpful. I thank her warmly and hope that she does not mind my having used them.

The Provost of Chelmsford, the Very Reverend H. M. Connop Price, has most kindly allowed a photograph of the Fitzwalter monument to be reproduced; and I am very grateful to the County Visual and Aural Aids Service for providing a copy. The Director-General's Department of the Greater London Council have generously supplied me with a print of Schomberg House from their *Survey of London, Volume XXX* and allowed me to reproduce it. For the other illustrations I am much indebted to the Essex Record Office and its photographers, Nelson Hammond and Jon Nutton.

INTRODUCTION

Family Background

Benjamin Mildmay, Earl Fitzwalter, and his immediate forbears sprang from a union of the ampelopsis and the yew. The Mildmays had long been sedulous social climbers. They were an old Gloucestershire family of no special note, first mentioned in Stephen's reign. They were connected, possibly as retainers, with the Marshal Earls of Pembroke and, later, with the de Bohuns and the Hollands. In the 15th century they were retainers of the Staffords, the Earls and Dukes of Buckingham. All these great families were inter-related.

Then a Walter Mildmay turned up in Essex as an officer in the household of the Duchess of Buckingham at Writtle and holder of lands in Great Waltham. In the early 16th century, his son, Thomas Mildmay I, illegally obtained a stall in Chelmsford market, prospered, acquired a house (now demolished) in the centre of the town, and became the founder of the Chelmsford, the main Essex, branch. This Thomas Mildmay (d. 1550) and his son, Thomas Mildmay II, Auditor of the Court of Augmentations, laid the basis of the family fortunes; at the Reformation they secured the rich, contiguous manors of Chelmsford (Bishop's Hall) and Moulsham. The Auditor began the building (or rebuilding) of Moulsham Hall, a handsome courtyard house, "then accounted the greatest esquire's building within the county of Essex". His son, Thomas Mildmay III, Sir Thomas Mildmay, completed the house. He married Frances Radcliffe, one of the daughters and co-heiresses of Henry Radcliffe, 2nd Earl of Sussex, of New Hall, Boreham, formerly Henry VIII's summer palace of Beaulieu. This was the union of the ampelopsis and the yew—the aspiring Mildmays and the Radcliffes, who were the heirs of the Fitzwalters, and the Fitzwalters had been at or near the heart of English history since Magna Carta and earlier; the Mildmays had arrived. By the end of the 16th century there were nine branches of the family in Essex alone;

and Sir Walter Mildmay of Apethorpe in Northamptonshire (d. 1589), Sir Thomas Mildmay's uncle, had been Elizabeth's Chancellor of the Exchequer and the founder of Emmanuel College, Cambridge, that crucible of the puritan temper.

When the main Radcliffe line died out in 1643, the earldom of Sussex became extinct, but the ancient and prestigious barony of Fitzwalter went into abeyance as between the descendants of those co-heiresses of the 2nd Earl of Sussex. This left a penultimate pinnacle for the aspiring Mildmays to climb. It was achieved in 1670, when Benjamin Mildmay's claim was upheld and he became the 17th Lord Fitzwalter. His son, Charles, succeeded him but died on February 16th, 1728, without issue, and was followed by his brother, Benjamin, who kept the accounts which are the subject of this book. In 1730, Benjamin ascended two steps in the peerage to become Viscount Harwich and Earl Fitzwalter. This was the ultimate pinnacle of the Mildmays' social ambition; he needed that earldom to maintain his dignity as the husband of George I's cousin and James I's great-grand-daughter.

He was born in 1672 and baptized at Chelmsford on December 27th. For the next fifty years very little is known about him—he rested in the quasi-obscurity appropriate to a younger son. From 1706 to 1708 he was equerry to Queen Anne's husband, Prince George of Denmark, of whom Charles II had said, "I have tried him drunk and tried him sober, and, odd's fish, there's nothing in the man." He was Chief Commissioner of the Salt Duties, 1714–20, and Commissioner of Excise, 1720–28. This last job was valuable to him: he seems to have used the Excise Office as a convenient bank. Until he was 51 he remained a bachelor, presumably a gay one, for, later, Horace Walpole referred to him as "an old beau".

Then the middle-aged bachelor fell in love, badly. She was Frederica Darcy, daughter of Meinhardt, Duke of Schomberg, grand-daughter of the famous Marshal Schomberg—"gallant old Schomberg" as Sir Winston Churchill called him—and widow of Robert, 3rd Earl of Holderness, with two small children, the 4th Earl and Lady Caroline Darcy. Her other (maternal) grandfather was Charles Louis, Elector Palatine, George I's uncle and the son of Frederick, the luckless "Winter King" of Bohemia, and Elizabeth Stuart, the "Queen of Hearts".

The match was commented on: it aroused the sharp-taloned wit of Lady Mary Wortley Montagu—

"Could anyone believe that Lady Holderness is a beauty, and in love? She is tenderly attached to the polite Mr. Mildmay and sunk in all the joys of happy love, notwithstanding she wants the use of her two hands by a rheumatism and he has an arm he cannot move. I wish I could send you particulars of the account, which seems to me as curious as that between two oysters and as well worth the serious enquiries of the naturalists."

But it was the real thing: the two oysters seem to have lived happily together for 27 years, and when her gout and rheumatic disorders finally killed her in August 1751, the old bivalve was heavily shaken, literally so, for the handwriting in his account book became tremulous.

If it were not for this marriage, nobody would ever know anything about Fitzwalter other than the bare bones of his career. The middle-aged swain began to keep those detailed illuminating accounts from his wedding day onwards. The very first four entries run
1724 "June 18

To Mr. Peres for my shaving-plate	...	...	...	...	£25 0s. 0d.
To a licence	...	...	...	£11 3s. 0d.
To Dr. Clarke (*the parson*)	...	£10 10s. 0d.
To the servants in family, drummers, etc.	...	...	...	£28 17s. 0d."

The next entry is not so relevant—
"To 11 load of old hay"

But, a little farther down is
"To two Common Prayer books £0 14s. 0d."

His marriage was the first of two outstanding events in his life. It brought him into close contact with the Royal Family. His wife's money augmented his own relatively modest income and enabled him to build up a useful fortune. Through her he became the proud occupant of a commodious town residence, Schomberg House in Pall Mall, remodelled a quarter of a century earlier by her father, Meinhardt, Duke of Schomberg and Leinster.

The second significant event in his life was his succession to the Fitzwalter peerage in 1728. It enabled him to return home and become an Essex magnate; it gave him a more elevated social position from which to advance his personal career. At the time of his brother's death he was living at Popes, near Hatfield, Herts, a modest house and very small estate, which he rented. Within three months he had bought Moulsham Hall from his brother's widow and immediately made preparations to rebuild it completely. Within another two months, on July 15th, 1728, he and his architect, Giacomo Leoni, saw Lady Fitzwalter lay a nominal first brick. The rebuilding was deliberately planned to be a piecemeal job spread out over the next twenty years or more. It obviously gave Fitzwalter a good deal of pleasure; so, too, did the furnishing and general embellishment of the place.

Fitzwalter was a firm supporter of the Hanoverian Succession. He was on fairly close terms with the Royal Family and with Walpole and the leading Whigs; thus it is not surprising that he was given public advancement. His earldom was granted in 1730. He became Chief Commissioner of the Board of Trade and Plantations in 1735, and Treasurer of the Household in 1737. In 1741 he was made Lord Lieutenant of Essex and Custos Rotulorum. There is little doubt that his Treasurership was the office which most suited him. It was not onerous—George II spent as much time as he could in Hanover—but it kept Fitzwalter in the Court circle and at the centre of public affairs. There was plenty of time left for him to play the landed magnate and watch Moulsham Hall being steadily brought to his *beau ideal* of a nobleman's country seat. The period from 1737 and all through the 1740s was a particularly congenial time for him, as, indeed, it was for all who were not poor, not sick in mind and body and not troubled by a social conscience—or any other kind of conscience! Later, Lady Fitzwalter's more frequent attacks of gout were painful and distressing. They necessitated many visits to Bath and Tunbridge Wells, occasional trips to the local spa at Islington and one long northern journey which included a 'cure' at Harrogate. But it is well-known that Georgian spas were not without their delights to distract visitors from their aches and pains.

Lady Fitzwalter died in 1751, aged 63; he died on February 29th, 1756, in his 84th year. He was buried in Chelmsford Cathedral and is commemorated by a handsome monument by James Lovell, later a protégé of Horace Walpole. His heir was his cousin, Sir William Mildmay, the diplomat, who died without issue in 1771. Meanwhile, the other branches of the Mildmay family were dying out; they were paying the penalty for their rapid rise—families whose members persistently marry heiresses add to their lands and their heraldic quarterings, but they sign their death warrant; it is life's law of diminishing returns. The last Essex male Mildmay was a member of Dr. Johnson's circle, old Carew Harvey Mildmay of Marks, Romford, who died in 1784. The last male Mildmay was Carew Mildmay of Shawford, Hants. His daughter, Jane, married Sir Henry Paulet St. John of Dogmersfield, Hants, who assumed the name of Mildmay. They had 12 children, and this new Mildmay family flourished for another century and a half.

The Account Books

Fitzwalter kept his own accounts in his own unmistakable hand. That is mainly why they are interesting: in those highly personalised entries the man himself keeps breaking through—

1748   March 6th
"Gave Dr. Beaumont for attending me five or six
times in order to remove a little complaint in one
of my eyes—veritable charlatan ...   . £4 4s. 0d."

Six account books have survived. Five are in the Essex Record Office; the sixth turned up in the Dogmersfield archives and is now in the Hampshire Record Office; one book is missing. The date range is 1724–54. The earlier books are composite; they accompanied him when he went from his town house to his country house and back again. Then Fitzwalter decided to have two current books, one for the town and one for the country. The catalogue number, dates and venue of his books are given in the following table—

(1) E.R.O., D/DM A4   June 1724–June 1726 — Composite book: Popes, Herts, and the London House.

(2) H.R.O., 15M 50/31   June 1726–Dec. 1732 — Begins as a composite book: at first, Popes and the London House; then, Moulsham Hall and the London House. From 1729 it is solely a London book.

(3) E.R.O., D/DM A5   Sept. 1729–May 1741 — Moulsham Hall book.
(4) E.R.O., D/DM A6   Dec. 1732–Dec. 1741 — London book.
(5) E.R.O., D/DM A7   Jan. 1742–Dec. 1752 — London book.
(6) E.R.O., D/DM A8   Jan. 1753–Dec. 1754 — London book.
                      (Missing book, 1742–?1754 — Moulsham Hall book.)

The loss of a Moulsham book (possibly, two volumes) is regrettable but not as serious as the loss of one of the two main London books (A6 and A7) would have been. As it is, the record for the years 1724–41 is very detailed. It is not a *complete* record since it does not include that part of the estate income and expenditure which passed through the hands of the steward. Moreover, a close examination of Fitzwalter's books shows that quite often he forgot to record items of expenditure, and sometimes he forgot to record items of income.

The form of the accounts has some bearing on their value as historical evidence. Fitzwalter's method of book-keeping should be a joy to anyone who could not tell a balance sheet from a profit-and-loss account! He would reserve a couple of pages at the beginning of a composite or London book for notes on his investments. Then he would simply enter his income on the left hand and his expenditure on the right hand pages. There was a drawback to this arrangement: his income usually arrived in large amounts at regular intervals, whereas his expenditure was a continuous stream of relatively small sums; thus the left hand page entries soon lagged far behind. But the blank pages were useful to Fitzwalter: the current account book was always somewhere near him, and the left hand pages provided him with space for comments, sometimes pungent, on the events which were uppermost in his mind. Not all comments, however, were left hand page entries; some of them, if they were short and certainly if they involved expenditure, went down on the right hand side.

The way in which the accounts have been prepared for publication calls for some explanation. Well over twenty years ago, before one of the missing books was discovered in the Dogmersfield archives, it was realised that those volumes in the Essex Record Office were far more interesting and illuminating than the average run of 18th century accounts but not sufficiently important to justify anyone undertaking a biography of Fitzwalter. This would have involved searching the central records for details of the public career of one who was never much more than a Whig placeman. It would have been unsuitable and very wasteful to print the books as they stood. The only sensible course was to publish extracts arranged under subjects and to preface each subject with a short explanatory narrative; in other words, to compile a source book. This method has not always been followed with uniformity. Some prefatory narratives are longer than others; some sets of extracts are much more drastically selective than others. The extracts relating to the rebuilding of Moulsham Hall, for instance, are numerous, because it is felt that an increasing number of people are interested in the *minutiae* of Georgian building. Sometimes, other documents have been brought in, such as one of Paul de Lamerie's rendered accounts and odd bills found loose in the account books. There is some variation, too, in the details of presentation. As the sets of extracts are mostly compiled from the six main account books, there did not seem to be any merit in frequently giving their catalogue numbers (shown on pages x-xi). For other extracts, the catalogue numbers *are* given. In some sets of extracts the spelling and punctuation have been modernised; in others the original spelling has been retained. In short, any charge of inconsistency will be readily and blandly admitted; the book is certainly no more than a Georgian ragbag, but, oh, what lovely fabrics the Georgians wore!

References

The summary of the pre-Essex history of the Mildmays is taken from unpublished essays by Valerie Cooper (Essex Record Office, T/Z 13/41, 57).

The reference to the first Thomas Mildmay was kindly supplied by Hilda Grieve.

The comment on the Auditor's Moulsham Hall comes from a survey, 1591, by John Walker, Senior. The survey has long been lost, but a portion of it was printed in Morant's *History of Essex*, II, p. 3, note F.

A list of offices held by Benjamin Mildmay, Earl Fitzwalter, is given in Sir Richard Colvin's *Lieutenants and Keepers of the Rolls of the County of Essex*.

A good deal of the rest of the *Introduction* is derived from *The Complete Peerage*, V, pp. 487–92 (under Fitzwalter).

The Account Books of

BENJAMIN MILDMAY

EARL FITZWALTER

CHAPTER ONE

"MY FAMILY"

When Fitzwalter referred to "my family" he nearly always used the term in its widest sense to mean everyone in the household, including the servants. Sometimes it referred to the servants only: in November 1751 he wrote

"Returned from Moulsham Hall to Pall Mall with my Lord and Lady Ancram and Louisa and brought up all my family".

Family

To his family in the narrower sense he was devoted. He was immediately solicitous for his wife when her minor indispositions and her recurrent severe illness struck her. He was obviously pleased that her kinship with the Royal Family brought her within the Royal circle. Occasionally his solicitude and pleasure can both be detected in one sentence

"To Dr. Hollings for Lady Fitzwalter's having a giddiness one night when she came home from play-ing with the Queen at the Dining Room   ...   ... £1 1s. 0d."

When they were married she was only 36 and he could look forward with confidence to founding a family. When he was rising 53 he wrote proudly, "my son was born August 27th, 1725, in the house in the Pall Mall a quarter of an hour before ten o'clock". But poor little Schomberg Mildmay lived only eighteen months. He seems to have suffered from a rupture, a fever due to teething

13

troubles and the after-effects of inoculation against small-pox. Sir Hans Sloane, two other doctors and an apothecary were in attendance, but they could not save him—even though they cut his gums and bled him just before he died! During the next few years Lady Fitzwalter had several miscarriages, but there were no more children for Fitzwalter.

This was a pity. He was regarded by the outside world as mean and covetous. Perhaps he *was* mean: his account books show that he watched his expenditure carefully; but they also show that he had a heart, especially for children. He was good to his stepson, Lord Holderness. He carried out the normal duties of a father: he sent the boy to Westminster School; he gave him adequate regular pocket-money, and more on special occasions; he paid all bills; he arranged for him to attend a good riding school and a fencing school; he sent him to Trinity Hall, Cambridge, and seems to have encouraged him to go on a modified Grand Tour. But he did more than his duty—he had a genuine concern for the boy; for instance, when Holderness developed an ague at Cambridge, he sent his steward there in his coach, accompanied by George Garnier, one of the leading London apothecaries.

He was obviously fond of his step-daughter, Lady Caroline Darcy. He provided her with the normal tutors—Siris, the dancing master; Ducaine, the writing master; Rolli who taught the spinet; and Martini, the singing master. But he kept an eye on these foreigners!—

1734, July 29th
"Pd. by the hands of my Lady Caroline Darcy to Signor Martini for teaching her to sing and play upon the harpsichord for 8 months, and is in full of all accounts to this day, and amounts (with the 3 guineas for entrance) to 27 guineas, for which he gave her a thing he called a receipt, writ in Italian, which in reality is no receipt, but is in her keeping, £28 7s. 0d."

He stopped Sir Thomas Robinson when he was just off to the Continent, handed him two guineas and asked him to bring back some memento for her from Paris.

When they grew up and married, he continued to follow their progress with pride and, sometimes, with concern. He lived to see his stepson become an ambassador and a secretary of state, and when Holderness was recalled from Venice in some disgrace, he recorded it in his account book, but in French to hide it from prying eyes.

Fitzwalter's stepson-in-law, the husband of Lady Caroline, was William Henry Kerr, Lord Ancram, later to be the 4th Marquis of Lothian and a very distinguished general. He served in Cumberland's army in the Netherlands and was wounded at Fontenoy. Then he rejoined Cumberland in time for the later part of the campaign against Prince Charles Edward. Fitzwalter followed the rigours and fortunes of the Forty-Five, and as the news came to him he wrote it in his account book—a running commentary, ending with Culloden and the trial of Simon Fraser, Lord Lovat. His account of Culloden has been published at least three times, but it is so vivid, so partisan, so immediate, so much the authentic raw material of history that it deserves another printing. (See chapter on *Public Affairs.*)

Fitzwalter took equal pride in the next generation, his stepchildren's children, particularly Lady Ancram's son and daughter, Lord Newbattle and Lady Louisa Kerr. Lord Ancram was so much on active service that it is almost certain that Lady Ancram continued to live with the Fitzwalters; certainly, her children were born in the Pall Mall house. Later, in Fitzwalter's last years, after the death of his wife, little Lady Louisa was his constant companion. He paid the bills for her clothes; he bought her a chamber organ and a harpsichord, a gold watch chain, a shagreen watch case, a "writing box" and some fishing tackle; he paid her tutors, including the Mr. Siris, who had been her mother's dancing master. He gave her a guinea a week pocket-money; this was plainly entered in the accounts, but when he bought little presents for her, he recorded this in what he felt was the obscurity of rather schoolboy French—

"Pour des bagatelles pour my Lady Louisa."

When the only son of the Earl and Countess of Holderness died, Fitzwalter was sad—

"The small-pox came out upon my Lord Darcy, September 19th, 1747, being then turned two year old. The poor child died, the 28th, being the 9th day. I never saw a finer or more promising boy."

Yes, Fitzwalter had a heart.

Servants

Fitzwalter's establishment did not change much throughout the period of the account books. At Schomberg House he kept

	£ per annum
Valer de chambre	12
Butler	15
Cook (man)	30–35
Hall porter	7
Footmen (usually five)	7 each
Coachman	10
2nd Coachman	6
Postillion	6
Housekeeper	10
Lady's maid	10
Chambermaid	6
Under cook (woman)	5
Town gardener	2

In addition there were two housemaids, Lady Caroline's maid and Lord Holderness's manservant. In due course, the wages of his stepchildren's servants ceased to be his responsibility. Occasionally he engaged an additional footman, and in 1750 he made a new appointment, a Groom of Chambers (£12). All servants lived in except the coachmen who were allowed 7s. a week board wages. Most servants travelled with him when he went to Moulsham or to other parts of the country; a few were then put on board wages. There were also several household servants, including a gardener (£10–20) and a dairymaid, kept at Moulsham, where his steward (£25) was based and, almost certainly, his groom and a stableboy.

Salaries remained fairly constant; there were few exceptions. When a new cook was appointed in 1746 the salary went up from £30 to £35. The postillion's wages were steadily advanced from £3 to £6. The coachman earned a good deal more than his £10, for he was paid for farrier's work and for maintaining coaches (see section on *Personal Transport*). He must have been tough and courageous—

1744   April 30

"Gave Mr. Broughton, the famous boxer, on fighting and beating the coachman, £1 1s. 0d."

The wages paid may seem small compared with those in some skilled trades. The real wages were much higher: service in a noble household meant a reasonably secure, well-ordered life, with plenty to eat, perhaps too much to drink, all occupational clothes provided and few personal expenses. The best servants stayed or left for honourable reasons, the idle or drunken were summarily dismissed; the sick were cared for; the dead were buried at Fitzwalter's cost, although if wages were owing to a dead servant he was not above using them as part payment for the funeral! Incidentally, when a servant left, whether for good or bad reasons, he was always "discharged" by Fitzwalter. For instance, Richard Plater, the Moulsham Hall gardener, was discharged by Fitzwalter. No reason is given in the account book; indeed, at the time of leaving, Plater was competently carrying out additional duties following the death of Dwinger, the steward. Moreover, he went on renting a hop ground and a public house from Fitzwalter, and seems to have remained on good terms with him.

Although establishment and wages were mainly stable, there was plenty of coming and going. Fitzwalter brought Edward Johnson, his butler, with him from Popes to Moulsham Hall, but when his steward, Nicholas Dwinger, died in 1733, he gave Johnson the job, an excellent choice. Then he ran into butler trouble. He sacked one in 1734 and another in 1735. He thought he had a good one in Edward Turner, but had to discharge him for drunkenness in 1738. He appointed John Longmore, promoted him to valet when Wilkins died in 1744, but sacked him in 1751. Longmore's successor as butler in 1744 was William Nutting, a footman; he stayed—he was manifestly reliable.

Footmen were frequently coming and going—going sometimes for honourable reasons, sometimes for idleness, dishonesty, drunkenness or nights on the tiles. There was little trouble between the sexes in the household itself, although Sarah Batten, one of the housemaids, did "run away after a butler I discharged"! He was Thomas Robson, described by Fitzwalter as "continually drunk, and a sot".

There were several instances of long service. Elizabeth Dwinger, the former steward's daughter, became housekeeper about 1731 and remained for over 20 years. Mrs. Jones, Lady Fitzwalter's personal maid, was there by March 1729. She survived her mistress and was still in the household on December 1st, 1753, when Dr. Pringle attended her for "a paralytic disorder". Thomas Garnham, the coachman, is first mentioned in 1729 but may well have entered Fitzwalter's service nearly two years earlier; he was probably still there when the account book series ends.

References

Some of the references to Lord Ancram come from *The Complete Peerage*, VIII, p. 153 (under *Lothian*).

John Broughton, the pugilist, was important enough to achieve a niche in the *Dictionary of National Biography*, and a memorial tablet (in Latin) in Lambeth Church.

Family—selective extracts

		£	s.	d.
1725	Oct. 13th			
	To Sir Hans Sloane for my son and Lady Caroline the day they were both inoculated	2	2	0
	Dec. 10th			
	To Mr. Nichols, one of the masters in Westminster School, for entrance money for Lord Holderness	5	5	0
1727	July 15th			
	To Mr. Arne, upholder, in part of his bill for the funeral charges of my son Schomberg of £36 15s. 0d. Paid	20	0	0
1729	Dec. 7th			
	To Mr. Ducaine, writing-master for Lady Caroline	3	16	0
	To Lady Caroline her quarter's allowance for gloves, ribbons, etc.	3	3	0
1730	May 21st			
	Pd. Mr. Siris, in part of a bill of £72 given in for learning Lord Holderness and Lady Caroline to dance	50	0	0
1731	Jan. 29th			
	Pd. Lady Caroline her Quarter due at Christmas last, and gave her half a guinea to buy her a fan	3	13	6

	£	s.	d.

Dec. 21st
Pd. Lady Caroline Darcy her half year's allowance to buy her own clothes, due Nov. 26th last past 50 0 0

1732 Aug. 1st
Pd. Signor G. Rolli in full for teaching Lady Caroline Darcy on the spinet ... 9 9 0

1733 Feb. 8th
To Signor Cori, Lady Caroline's Italian master, for entrance, one guinea and a half, and for one month's teaching ending this day, the same 3 3 0

1734 Jan. 15th
To the expenses of plays and operas for my Lord Holderness 2 2 0

Feb. 9th
To Mr. Serjeant Dickens for the use of his brother, the professor, the sum of £58 8s. 4½d., being in full for bills due at Cambridge to the 21st of Dec. last past on account of the Earl of Holderness; and paid him also £25 for the use of the said professor for his year's salary, ending the 19th of November last past as tutor to the Earl of Holderness 84 8 4½

Mar. 14th
For my (*Lady*) Caroline's chair on the wedding day of the Prince of Orange and the following days 3 3 0

May 10th
Sent my coach to Cambridge for my Lord Holderness upon his having an ague there. Sent Mr. G. Garnier, the apothecary, and my steward for him. Spent on the road in going and coming in three days 5 15 6

July 29th
Paid by the hands of my Lady Caroline Darcy to Signor Martini for teaching her to sing and play upon the harpsichord for

	£	s.	d.

July 29th—*cont.*

8 months, and is in full of all accounts to this day, and amounts (with the 3 guineas for entrance) to 27 guineas, for which he gave her a thing he called a receipt, writ in Italian, which in reality is no receipt but is in her keeping   28   7   0

1735 Jan. 13th

Paid Mr. H. Smart, lace man, for a broad, silver trimming, etc., for my Lady Caroline's petticoat, when she held up the train of the Princess Royal at her marriage with the Prince of Orange, March 1733 ...   75   17   6

Feb. 14th

Paid Mr. Hyde for carrying my Lord Holderness with a coach and six horses to Aston in the north in August last, and being out with him 15 days, which is in part of a bill delivered in of £35 12s. 6d.   24   7   6

June 7th

To Sir Thos. Robinson, who was going to Paris, to be laid out there for something for my Lady Caroline   2   2   0

Nov. 9th

To my Lady Fitzwalter to pay the house bills. N.B. My Lady Caroline Darcy was the 6th instant married to the Earl of Ancram, son to the Marquess of Lothian   60   0   0

Dec. 13th

Paid Mons. Bouée, valet de chambre to my Lord Ancram for 2 wigs and bags for my Lord Holderness   4   4   0

15th

Gave Mr. Foubert, by the hands of my Lord Holderness, entrance for his riding there, 4 guineas, to his equerry, one, and to the grooms, one, in all   6   6   0

		£	s.	d.
1736	Dec. 13th			
	Paid Mons. Murene, my Lord's fencing master, for 2 months from the 18th of October last to this day for himself and provost	3	3	0
1737	Apr. 4th			
	Paid Thos. Heath for a set of 6-inch, full size case of mathematical instruments for the Earl of Holderness	4	16	6
1738	May 26th			
	Paid Signor Cori, Italian language master, for entrance and teaching the Earl of Holderness 2 months, and in full ...	6	6	0

post Aug. 1st

Memorandum. The Earl of Holderness set out from my house in the Pall Mall, May 17th 1738, for Paris, where he stayed till the French King went to Compeigne; then followed the Court thither, stayed there a week, and from there set out for Dover and came cross the country by way of Gravesend, and arrived here the 24th of July. Stayed here till the first of August. Then I carried him as far as Colchester in his way to Harwich, where he embarked for Holland, where he proposes to look about him and see what is to be seen in that part of the world for 2 months. Then, to return by way of Lille to Fontainebleau, and from thence to Paris, and there to pass his winter.

		£	s.	d.
1739	Dec. 21st			
	Gave the nurses for the christening of my Lady Ancram's daughter (*Lady Louisa*) when I stood godfather	10	10	0
1743	Sept. 22nd			

My Lord Ancram returned this day to London from the army in Germany, after having stayed 2 months at Aix-la-Chapelle in hopes of getting (*rid*) of his rheumatic

Sept. 22nd—*cont.*   £ *s. d.*

pains, which (*he*) contracted to a very
great degree in the Camp, and came home
very ill.

1744   May 1st

The Earl of Holderness, then a Lord of the
Bedchamber, kissed the King's hand as
Ambassador to Venice, being then not
quite six-and-twenty year old.

1746   Mar. 18th

Les lettres de rappel de la Comte de Holderness de son ambassade à Venise furent
envoye d'ici par le Duc de Newcastle le
15th de ce mois de Mars, 1745.

1747   Feb. 2nd

Returned to London from Bath with my
Lady Fitzwalter and my Lord and my
Lady Ancram, who had been there with
us a month, besides my Lord and my
Lady Holderness, who came down and
stayed with us above a fortnight. My own
family consisted also of fifteen in number.
I had also there fifteen horses, and from
my setting out from this place to my
return was eleven weeks, in which expedition I spent (sending down 16 dozen of
my own wine)   366   0   0

post Sept. 10th

My Lord Newbattle was put to Eton School
the 9th or 10th of this inst. Sept., 1747.

post Sept. 28th

The small-pox came out upon my Lord
Darcy, Sept. 19th, 1747, being then turned
two year old. The poor child died the 28th
being the 9th day. I never saw a finer or
more promising boy.

		£	s.	d.
1749	May 24th The Earl of Holderness set out with my Lady from Moulsham Hall to Harwich in his way for Holland, to which place he is sent to reside as Minister Plenipotentiary from the King of England to the States-General.			
1752	Jan. 1st Paid Mr. Siris, dancing master for my Lady Louisa Kerr, in full for one month ending yesterday	2	7	0
	27th Paid for a chamber organ for my Lady Louisa	5	5	0
	Feb. 17th Paid Mons. Gracieux, drawing master for my Lady Louisa, this month in full ...	2	2	0
1753	Jan. 3rd Paid Mr. Gray for a gold chain for Lady Louisa's watch	5	5	0
	11th Paid Mr. Gray and partner for a shagreen watch-case for my Lady Louisa ...	1	1	0
	Feb. 12th Monfradini, music master, gave my Lady Louisa her first lesson, March 23rd, paid him for entrance, £3 3s. 0d., and also £3 3s. 0d. N.B. his second month begins March 12th	6	6	0
	June 9th Pour des bagatelles pour my Lady Louisa...	1	9	0
1754	Feb. 20th Paid my Lady Ancram's bills in full for my Lady Louisa's new clothes and other necessaries	42	0	6
	May 1st Paid for a harpsichord for my Lady Louisa	25	0	0

Servants—selective extracts £ *s. d.*

1733 Dec. 7th
Paid Edward Johnson, my butler, his yearly
wages in full as a butler, due from the 2nd
of February last past to 24th June, 1733.   4 15 0
N.B. his yearly wages as steward then
begin at £25 *per annum.*

1734 May 10th
Discharged and paid off Thos. Robson, my
butler, his yearly wages and all accounts,
in full to this day 3 6 0
N.B., this Robson was continually drunk,
and a sot.

May 17th
Paid Sarah Battan a year's wages due to her
when she ran away after a butler I discharged. Query, if any more is due to her.
N.B. She would not take it till all was
paid 5 0 0
(struck through)

June 20th
Paid Sarah Burton (*Battan*), a servant maid
discharged, her yearly wages in full being
about a year and half 7 6 0

1735 Feb. 18th
Paid off and discharged Wm. Shenton, my
gardener, his yearly wages due to him for
7 months at £20 *per annum,* paid in full   11 15 0
N.B. A very lazy, idle fellow. N.B. Hired
Peter le Dean, a Frenchman, at the same
wages; sent him down to Moulsham, 17th
inst.

Sept. 20th
Paid Edward Turner, my butler, his half
year's wages due 16th July last past and
which is £6 0s. 0d., and at the same time
gave him a guinea, having served me well   7 1 0

1736 Mar. 25th   £ *s.* *d.*
Paid "Duchess", my undercook, her yearly
wages in full to this day from 2nd of
February last, and discharged her, that
she might go and serve my Lady Ancram   16 0

April 27th
Discharged Jeremy Harrison, a footman,
who had lived with me about 6 months.
He pretended a quarrel with Wilkins, my
valet de chambre, and desired to be gone.
He is a surly, idle, lazy, lying fellow. Paid
him his wages in full 1 7 6

1736 May 18th
Paid John Binks, the servant that belongs to
the Earl of Holderness, his year's wages
due and in full to April 3rd, 1737   ...   12 0 0

1737 Jan. 10th
Paid off and discharged Samuel Bowling, a
footman that had served me about 8
months and left me to go upon the stage.
N.B. a quiet, sober fellow. Paid him in
full 5 0 0

1739 June 21st
Paid Charles Turner, a footman, that lived
with me 7 years, his yearly wages in full,
and turned him over to the Earl of
Holderness. N.B. he is a good, sober
fellow 2 14 6

1740 Feb. 21st
Paid Thos. Carr and Wm. Fargue for nursing and burying Edward Stouton, my postillion, the sum of four pounds, ten shillings, which was more than his wages

	£	s.	d.

Feb. 21st—*cont.*

came to by £1 12s. 0d., his wages being
five pounds *per annum*, due February 2nd,
1739/40, of which I had advanced him
£2 2s. 0d. 4 10 0

1741 Apr. 15th

Gave my Lord Holderness's cook for help-
ing mine last week and to-day, when Sir
Robert Walpole and the Duke of Grafton,
with many others, dined with me   ...   2 2 0

1742 Jan. 20th

Paid Longmore, my butler, his bill in full for
going down with others to Gravesend to
seize a thief that stole a silver dish out of
my house. N.B. They found the dish and
the man on board an East India ship.
They brought him up to Town, and I had
him condemned of felony 1 0 4

Mar. 22nd

Paid for the lodgings and diet of Luke, one
of my footmen, at Chelsea after he had
had the measles, £0 8s. 6d., and also for
his nurse and lodgings in Town during
the time he had them, £1 1s. 0d. 1 9 6

1743 April 29th

Paid Luke Crawforth, one of my footmen,
in full for his yearly wages to 2nd of May
next. An unhealthy, but a very good,
honest servant. Discharged him 1 15 0

May 2nd

Gave Luke Crawforth, my footman, to carry
him to his friends in Yorkshire 2 2 0

		£	s.	d.

1744 April 9th
    Paid for the funeral of Wilkins, my valet de
      chambre 7 18 1

1746 Nov. 10th
    Paid — Roberts, my cook, his yearly wages
    in full, due to him the 2nd of this inst.
    Nov., being 3 quarters of a year,
    £22 10s. 0d. Gave him, also, £1 1s. 0d., the
    man being by ill-health incapable to serve
    me any longer, having (*been*) in my service
    about twenty years 23 11 0

1747 Dec. 22nd
    Paid Charles Woollam, a discharged foot-
    man, his wages in full; an idle, stupid,
    drunken, good-for-nothing fellow ...   2 19 6

CHAPTER TWO

THE REBUILDING OF MOULSHAM HALL

On May 17th, 1728, thirteen weeks after his brother's death, Fitzwalter bought Moulsham Hall, with 45 acres around it, for £630 from his sister-in-law, the dowager Lady Fitzwalter. Probably it was substantially the 16th century house, begun by Thomas Mildmay the Auditor, completed by his son, Sir Thomas, and faithfully depicted by John Walker on his map of 1591—a two-storeyed timbered house around the innermost of three courtyards, with a one-storeyed wing running off to the north.

Fitzwalter planned his new house with characteristically cautious prudence. It was to be a long-term project, so that the payments for its various phases did not run ahead of the steady increase in his personal wealth. There was no rash, wholesale demolition: beginning with the south front, one wing at a time was pulled down; the foundations were used for the new work, and no more demolition was undertaken until the new work was well-advanced. The Tudor courtyard was reduced in size by a four-sided corridor with gallery above, giving independent access to all rooms. He employed Giacomo Leoni as his architect, but the finished result was nearer Wren in spirit than most of Leoni's achievements. Gandon's side-stretched, blind-eyed print is the best surviving representation of it, but is woefully inadequate. Its reasonable size, its fine proportions, its firm restraint relieved by rich carving, and that delightful contrast of red brick and Portland stone gave Fitzwalter just the kind of dignified home he required. It belonged to an age which had become elegant without ceasing to be robust.

Fitzwalter was at Moulsham Hall within three weeks of buying the place; almost certainly Leoni was with him. He was back again in July, when, on the 15th, he paid Leoni £21 for the plan and tipped the bricklayers 2 guineas when he and Lady Fitzwalter laid a nominal first brick. On August 8th he gave the carpenters a guinea when he and his wife drove home the first pin on the South front.

It is clear that right from those early days the supplies were flowing in smoothly. Bricks were supplied by Thomas Spite whose kilns were on Galleywood Common. Timber from the East London merchants came by water to Maldon. Quite early on there is a payment of £59 2s. for 113 tons of Portland stone. Presumably from the beginning and for as long as 12 years, Anthony Goude of Chelmsford, who built Terling church tower, was the stonemason.

The South front was up and roofed by the end of October 1729, and work was well in progress on the next section, for, on September 26th, Fitzwalter drove a nominal first pin into the carpenters' work in the main, East front. On November 11th he paid William Mantle, the plasterer, the first instalment on a bill for £17 15s., presumably for work in the South range. Possibly, John Boson, the Greenwich stone carver, was still working outside in the cold; at least, he did not receive until January 21st his final payment for the 40 guineas he charged for carving Fitzwalter's arms over the hall door. Meanwhile, Robert Mason of Chelmsford, the master painter, plumber and glazier, was hard at work inside, and so, too, were William Mantle and Anthony Goude.

About this time, too, work was in progress re-laying the gardens. In January 1730, Mr. Greening, the nurseryman, was paid £32 13s. 8d. for plants supplied and 6 guineas for going down four times to Moulsham Hall to give advice. In April, Fitzwalter paid a farmer 24 guineas for the carriage of 8 loads of trees which Greening had sent to Moulsham. By October 1730, Greening's bill amounted to £171 19s.

During the first two years of building, Fitzwalter would come down and stay from time to time. But by May 1730, the interior of the building was sufficiently finished for him to make a state entry; this was a particularly appropriate time, as the 19th baron Fitzwalter had just become Viscount Harwich and Earl Fitzwalter.

"Came to Moulsham Hall, May 22nd, 1730, in order to settle my family here for the summer."

The news had spread around in good time: as he passed by, the bells of Ingatestone and Widford churches greeted him, and each team of ringers received half a guinea. At Chelmsford there was almost a royal reception—

"Spent £10 4s. at the Saracen's upon my neighbours who came to meet me, being the minister and principal inhabitants of the town to the number of between 130 and 140 on horseback."

Simple arithmetic makes this about 1s. 6d. a head, and one could drink quite a good health for 1s. 6d. in 1730. A fortnight later he took his oath as churchwarden; and, apart from a few journeys to Town, he was at Moulsham Hall for the greater part of the rest of the year. During August, he was visited for 16 days by his sister-in-law, Lady Mary, and her husband, Count Dagenfeldt, the Prussian Minister.

But the two wings were far from completed. Robert Mason, the painter, John Dowyer the carver and his lame brother, James, and William Mantle, the plasterer, were all busy. So, too, were the labourers in the gardens and Great Court. A fireplace from Cheere and Scheemakers, the famous firm of sculptors, had to be fixed. In November 1730, the scaffolders erected Samuel Carpenter's 3 lead statues of Apollo, Diana and Mercury over the main pediment. As soon as Fitzwalter went back to Town on November 25th, if not earlier, the Italian plasterer, Bagutti, and his assistant, Artari, were at work on the ceilings. By January 1731, Bagutti had already been paid £161 8s., as well as a little bill of £1 15s. for painting the stucco dining room in water colours. Long before that time, the new furniture and fittings were being installed, and Samuel Boler, the cabinet maker, was running up his succession of long bills. Lancaster Noone, the Chelmsford upholsterer, was given plenty of work, and in January 1731, Lady Fitzwalter finished her task of supervising the embroidery of the red furniture in the East bed-chamber. Baker, the locksmith in Queen Square, Ormonde Street, had sent down locks costing £14 11s.

Throughout 1731 the work went on, mainly consolidating work. In April, Samuel Carpenter's men placed the leaden Mildmay lions on the great piers of the gateway. John Bagley, the carpenter, was making the "palisadoes" for the Great Court; the Great Court itself was sown with grass seed; the fine iron gates by Montigny, costing £50, were erected. Pictures* by the Venetian, Jacopo Amigoni, were sent down from London. Dick Eves, the bricklayer, was building the interminable kitchen garden wall—Thomas Spite made 101,300 bricks in 1731. Thomas Ayling, stonemason, who also did work at the Pall Mall house, made a grand chimney-piece of Plymouth marble. Samuel Boler in London, and other crafts-

*All extracts relating to pictures mentioned in this chapter are given in the chapter on *Entertainment and the Arts*.

men on the site, were still busy; and, probably in April or May, Enoch Seeman's new, full-length portrait of Fitzwalter was finished and placed in the frame which Gousset had carved.

Then, probably in May, 1732, work began on the West front, Dick Eves pulled down the old Tudor brickwork, John Bagley dismantled the timbering, and Eves cleared the foundations. Eves got to work on the new brickwork and Goude on the stonework; and soon Robert Bernard, the carpenter, and George Gainge, the joiner, were following behind them. Meanwhile, the supplies were pouring in—bricks from Spite's kilns; lime from John Roper of Grays and Lawrence of Maldon; deals from John Cox, the Quaker, of Stratford, and other timber from Eeles and Courthorpe; locks and other ironwork from Stephen Lum of Chelmsford and brass locks from William Banks, the Quaker.

By the late autumn, the outside work was done, and the water supply (through elm pipes of 6-inch bore) was laid on from the Conduit Field. William Fearnley, William Mantle's successor, could then get on with the plastering, using the laths supplied by Thomas Cass. Goude could pave the kitchen with Purbeck stone. George Gainge could carry on with the joinery; this was completed by August 6th, 1733. Dick Eves could get back to his everlasting kitchen garden wall.

Throughout 1733, 1734 and early 1735, there was little actual building but a good deal going on. Robert Mason was still gilding and doing other work. William Waters supplied framed mirrors; Scheemakers sent down the chimney-piece for the dining room; Bolar and Noone were still busy. Leoni was often coming down, earning his £100 a year; in November 1733 he was robbed of 3 guineas, for which Fitzwalter compensated him. There was considerable activity in the gardens—walks were being made and lined with elms; the mount was removed and a new one made; John Bagley was erecting rails and making garden furniture; seeds were being sent down by Samuel Gray of Pall Mall; Richard Dobson of Clapham supplied over three pounds' worth of Dutch and English anemones, jonquils, double pinks, carnations and polyanthuses.

In the summer of 1735, work began on the new stables, with the same craftsmen as before, except that Richard Eves was discharged and his place taken by John Middleton, and Robert Mason, the plumber, was replaced by John Blatch. Lead was costly even then: Blatch's bill came to £117 18s. 9d. for sheet lead and £39 4s. 0d.

for pipes, cisterns and hipping lead. Work on the stables was not finished until well into 1737. On July 27th, Bishop, the Bedford-shire carpenter, received his final payment for setting up and framing the cupolas. Even later, the famous clockmaker, Langley Bradley, was paid for erecting the stable clock and for providing a bell and two weather-vanes.

More work in the gardens was carried out in the winter of 1737–38. A new walk was made and lined with 40 elm trees and 300 hedge elms supplied by Edward Bolton of Ilford. A ha-ha was constructed in the proper manner, with a good retaining wall. A dog kennel was built.

In April 1739, Fitzwalter went down to Moulsham Hall with Leoni to mark out the foundations of the new brewhouse and dairy. The brewhouse was set in hand immediately, and work was begun on the dairy, laundry and wash-house on July 16th; thus, the work was well spaced, so that Gainge, the joiner, could move along behind Middleton, the bricklayer, without any hold-up. The external work, except the roofing, was finished by mid-August, but there was still work inside for Gainge and for Blatch, the painter. Indeed, the whole undertaking, together with the pigeon house and poultry yard, was not completed until September 1740.

Meanwhile, Fitzwalter was still steadily adorning his mansion. Andrea Soldi painted portraits of Lord Holderness and Lord Ancram to be hung in oval frames at the Hall. At the Smyrna Coffee House, Fitzwalter bought a painting of Childers, the Duke of Devonshire's famous racehorse. William Waters made a gilt frame and packed it carefully for its journey to Moulsham. Fitz-walter exchanged an inlaid bureau for a marble slab in a gilt frame and sent it down to the Hall. He paid £12 17s. 0d. to Thomas Heath, mathematical instrument-maker, for a horizontal brass dial-plate for the court in front of the house. More trees and plants were purchased for the gardens.

This is nearly the end of the story, as far as it can be traced in any detail. The Moulsham account book ends on April 28th, 1741. There must have been at least one more Moulsham book covering the period from 1741 down to 1754, when Fitzwalter, towards the end of his life, gave up keeping accounts. As far as the *building* is concerned, the missing book is not a catastrophic loss. Most of it was completed by 1741—three sides of the main house, the domestic offices, the grounds and the gardens.

Moulsham Hall in Essex the Seat of S.r W.m Mildmay Bar.t

The London accounts continue to show how Fitzwalter went on adorning the mansion he regarded with such pride. Occasionally, too, they show payments or memoranda relating directly to construction work—

"May 8th, 1743. Go this day to Moulsham to see the foundation laid for the North front, laid in order to the finishing of the whole building, Mr. Leoni having been there ever since the 5th inst. May."

Leoni continued to supervise the building, but that impoverished genius was soon to find existence made even more frugal—

"July 10th, 1744. Paid Mr. James Leoni the sum of £15 10s. 0d., which, with £84 10s. 0d. which he has received from me since May 4th, 1743, makes the complete sum of £100, and is in full to the 4th of May, 1744, for surveying my new building at Moulsham Hall. N.B. This agreement is not to continue for the current year, being determined not to give him more than £50."

The work continued: Eeles was still supplying timber; Samuel Gray was still sending down seeds. But new names were appearing, Richards was now the stone carver; Boson died in 1743. Goude died in 1741, and his place as stonemason was taken by William Cooley, and Cooley, in turn, was succeeded by Thomas Carver. The new wing contained the Great Room, 50 by 25 feet, with its elaborate ceiling, executed in 1745–6 by Artari. There were still a few years to go: the phrasing of occasional entries in the London book suggests that the building was not completed until the early weeks of 1749.

The total cost will never be known, even if the missing account book turned up; there are no later steward's account books surviving, and a number of composite entries by Fitzwalter cannot be broken down. An expenditure of about £12,000 is recorded before the North front was begun; maybe the total cost was around £17,000. Anyhow, it was never intended to be enormous or ostentatious, certainly not a Blenheim or a Castle Howard. Fitzwalter was the quintessence of the Age of Common Sense. He did not want a palace; he wanted a dignified, reasonably commodious home.

The rest of the house's brief history is known in outline. Fitzwalter's cousin and heir, Sir William Mildmay, succeeded him and lived there, and after he died in 1771 his widow continued to occupy the house. Eventually, Moulsham Hall and the vast possessions of all the Mildmay branches in Essex and elsewhere came to

the ultimate heiress, Jane Mildmay of Shawford, Hants. She and her
husband had little interest in Moulsham Hall. In the Napoleonic
wars it was occupied by the military, and the military have rarely
been regarded as sensitive custodians of architectural gems. Moreover, Chelmsford and its environs formed the northern hub of the
defences of London in case Napoleon should choose the long sea
route to the Suffolk and north Essex coast, and the anti-invasion
fortifications all along the Galleywood-Widford ridge spoilt the
amenities of the Hall. In 1809, it was pulled down. The traffic on
the by-pass now rushes rudely past its ghost, and all that was left
of Fitzwalter's building was his kitchen garden wall; and even that
was destroyed a few years ago.

References
   Walker's map, 1591, showing Old Moulsham Hall, is in the Essex Record
Office (D/DM P2).
   Some references to the last years of Leoni's Moulsham Hall are given
on p. 59 of *The Ancient Sepulchral Monuments of Essex* by Frederic
Chancellor. The book also gives a useful genealogical table of the Mildmays.

Rebuilding of Moulsham Hall—selective extracts

		£	s.	d.
1728	May 17th			
	Given to Merchant Morley upon my signing the deed of purchase of Moulsham Hall and 45 acres of land about it, of my sister Fitzwalter	21	0	0
	Paid to my Lady Dowager Fitzwalter for the said purchase, with the sole right of the game and making my gamekeepers in the manor of Moulsham and Chelmsford	630	0	0
	July 15th			
	To Mr. Leoni for his plan for building my house at Moulsham Hall	21	0	0
	To the bricklayers at Moulsham for my wife and I laying a brick	2	2	0
	Aug. 8th			
	To the carpenters for driving a peg in the building of Moulsham Hall	1	1	0

	£	s.	d.

Aug. 25th
    Paid to Mr. Leoni on account and in part of our agreement of six per cent for my building at Moulsham Hall   10   10   0

Nov. 29th
    To John Cox, Quaker near Bow, for 200 $\frac{3}{4}''$ of clean second deals, bought by Mr. Gainge, joiner, for my use. Paid in full...   25   14   3

1729 June 1st
    Sent Mr. Beard by letter a bank bill into the country of £100, which he received and is to pay Mr. Coe of Maldon for timber and freight of stone for my building   100   0   0

12th
    Left with Peniston Lamb of Lincoln's Inn . . . a bank bill of six hundred pounds to answer any bills my steward in Essex might (*have*) drawn upon him, during my being at Tunbridge, for carrying on my building in Essex.

Sept. 5th
    Advanced Mr. Beard, my steward, for Mr. Goude the stone mason   30   0   0

13th
    Accounted with Mr. Lamb for £600, which I had left in his hands . . . during my being at Tunbridge, and his account is as follows, viz: To Mr. Farrer, £105 which (*he*) paid to Mr. Charles Beard towards carrying (*on*) my building   105   0   0

    To Mr. Tucker and Gilbert, June 24th, for 113 ton of Portland stone sent to Maldon for my building   59   2   0

    To Mr. Lewis, Excise Collector for Essex, July 26th, £300, which he had advanced to Mr. Beard for carrying on my building, and repaid to the Commissioners of Excise   300   0   0

	£	s.	d.
Sept. 13th—*cont.*			
To Mr. Leoni, my architect, August 23rd, advanced	30	0	0
To Mr. Lewis, aforesaid, £100, advanced to Mr. Beard and repaid to the Commissioners of Excise	100	0	0
Sept. 26th			
To my carpenters for driving a pin in building the East front	1	1	0
27th			
To the joiners the same	1	1	0
29th			
To Symonds, one of the Maldon hoymen, in part of 50s. for bringing down 4,500 glazed tiles, there being some demands on him for quitrent, etc.	1	15	0
Oct. 2nd			
Advanced to Mr. Beard, on account of the building, which he paid to Mr. Mason, the plumber	30	0	0
4th			
To Richard, Mr. Greening's man, at 12s. per week, and 5 labourers in making my kitchen garden at 7s. per week	2	7	0
10th			
To John Barnes, clerk of the brick kilns at Brentwood, for 1,000 tiles	3	0	0
16th			
To one of the carpenters who was hurt here on the building		10	6
16th			
To a stone cutter who was hurt		5	0
30th			
Advanced to Mr. Charles Beard in order to pay off the workmen upon the admeasurement of my house, it being covered in, all the outside finished, Oct. 28th–29th. Measured by Mr. Burningham from London	200	0	0

	£	s.	d.

Nov. 6th

To Mr. Pullen (*surveyor*) in full for his trouble in looking (*after*) my affairs relating to the building for one year last past, etc. **7   7   0**

11th

Paid Mr. Mantle in full of a bill for plasterer's work, done for me at Moulsham Hall, of £74 15s., forty-one pound ten shillings thereof having been paid before ...   **33   5   0**

22nd

Paid to Richard and labourers for the kitchen garden and other works, 2 weeks ending this day **3 19   6**

29th

To the labourers about the house, Richard being gone **1   3   0**

Dec. 17th

Paid Mr. Leoni in further part on account of my building at Moulsham Hall   ...   **50   0   0**

18th

To Mr. Burningham for coming to Moulsham, staying ten days and measuring my house, and expenses on the road in going and coming **11 11   0**

20th

To Mr. Macreth, lime-man, in full for 4,500 glazed Dutch tiles for Moulsham Hall, and for lighterage, labourers, etc.   ...   **28 10   0**

1730   Jan. 17th

Paid Mr. Greening, the gardener, his bill in full, £32 13s. 8d., and for his trouble and expenses in going down four times himself, and his son once, to Moulsham Hall, £6 6s., in all **38 19   8**

	£	s.	d.
Jan. 21st			
To Mr. Boson, stone carver, for carving my coat of arms over the hall door at Moulsham Hall, being in the country, £17 5s., and now £24 15s., makes in all, £42, which is in full	24	15	0
March 10th			
Paid Mr. Mason of Chelmsford on account of materials and work done at Moulsham Hall in painting, plumbing and glazing as by bills given in amounting to about £114 in the whole, and out of which I shall deduct £5 or £6. I say, I have this day paid	100	0	0
Apr. 11th			
Advanced Mr. Beard to carry on my building etc.	100	0	0
And about the beginning of the same month advanced Mr. Beard one hundred pound more on the same account ...	100	0	0
21st			
To John Westbrooke, a farmer, who Mr. Greening employed to carry for me eight load of trees to Moulsham Hall from Brentford at 3 guineas per load. Paid him in full	25	4	0
May 5th			
Paid Mr. Goude, stone mason, for materials and work done at my house at Moulsham Hall, the sum of ninety-four pounds, which with £90 before paid by Mr. Beard, is in full for his bill of £184 7s. 0d.	94	0	0
22nd			
Came to Moulsham Hall, Friday, May 22nd, 1730, in order to settle my family here for the summer.			
Spent at Romford		10	6
Gave the ringers at Ingatestone		10	6

	£	s.	d.

May 22nd—*cont.*

Spent at the Saracen's upon my neighbours who came to meet me, being the Minister and principal inhabitants of the town to the number of between 130 or 140 on horseback 10 4 0

June 4th

Paid Dwinger his bill and board wages in full to today, with half a guinea for the ringers at Widford on my coming down, May 22nd 2 10 0

Oct. 1st

Paid Mr. Greening, nurseryman, in further part of his bill of £171 19s., having paid him August last £50 ... ... 60 0 0

16th

Advanced Mr. Carpenter, statuary, in part of £63 for 3 leaden statues which I am to pay him for them when they are delivered 10 10 0

17th

Paid to Courthorpe and Eeles, timber merchants, in part of a bill of £267 5s. 2d.... 150 0 0

22nd

Paid Mr. Mason for painting the principal storey and the garrets and my dressing-room and two attics at 6d. per yard, and 2 rooms in the old buildings at 4d. per yard, in all 1852 yards, his bill in full paid 62 0 0

27th

Paid Mr. Dowyer, the carver (the lame one), on account, as by receipt 6 6 0

29th

Advanced Mr. Beard £200 in bank bills to carry on my affairs, but two days after he paid me back £100 in gold, so that there remains for him to account for of those bills but £100 ... ... 100 0 0

Nov. 3rd   £   s.   d.
Paid Mr. Humphreys, brazier at Chelms-
ford, by the hands of Johnson, my butler,
for the frame of a lanthorn for the stair-
case, 8s., and for six brass nozzles at 2s.
apiece, in all   1   0   0

6th
Paid Mr. Mantle, plasterer, in part of a bill
delivered in this day of £217 4s. I say,
paid £50 bank bill and ten guineas   ...   60 10   0

7th
Paid the labourers in the Great Court and
gardens   5   4   2

11th
Paid Mr. Dowyer the carver's bill in full of
£101 9s. 4d., Mr. Beard having advanced
to his brother £74 11s. Paid also to his
brother by my own hands, £6 6s. Deducted also from the said bill as being overcharged and contrary to agreement made
between him and myself, £15, and paid
him now in full satisfaction of said bill as
by Mr. Dowyer's receipt, £5 8s. 6d.   ...   5   8   6

19th
Bought and paid for a brass outside lock of
Mr. Banks by the hands of Mr. Gainge
for the closet in the S.E. bedchamber   ...   14   0

20th
Paid Richard Hill and Peter Patrick, scaffolders, at 5s. per day, 16 days, for coming from London, setting up and taking
down the scaffold for erecting the statues   4   0   0

28th
Paid Mr. Carpenter in further part of his
three statues sent down to Moulsham Hall
in Essex   20   0   0

		£	s.	d.

Nov. 30th

Paid Mr. Carpenter, statuary, in full satisfaction for his 3 statues, £31 9s. which,
with what he received before, amounts
to £63 ... ...   31 9 0

Dec. 7th

Paid Mr. Bagutti, the Italian *stuccatore,* for
work by agreement he and Mr. Artari did
at Moulsham Hall for which is to have
£150, having paid him before £10 10s.
Paid this day £100... ... ...   100 0 0

15th

Paid Mr. Barker, locksmith, in Queen's
Street, his bill in full for locks sent down
to Moulsham Hall 14 14 0

1731 Jan. 2nd

Paid H. Cheere and H. Scheemakers, part-
ners and carvers, for a stone chimney piece
carved, £23, and for two marble slabs, all
for Moulsham, and in full 33 10 0

18th

Paid Mr. Bagutti for painting the stucco
dining room in watercolours 1 15 0

29th

Paid my wife in full for the work she has
paid for embroidering the red furniture in
the East bedchamber at Moulsham. I
say, paid my Lady Fitzwalter for all the
hired work 25 0 0

Feb. 13th

Having (*paid*) Mr. Bagutti, the Italian *stuccatore* for his work done in my hall and
dining room at Moulsham,   £115 15s.
I have this day also paid him   £45 13s.
                 ―――――――

which in the whole amounts to £161 8s.
which (is) in full for all the work Mr.
Artari and he have done for me to this

	£	s.	d.

Feb. 13th—*cont.*
  day. My agreement was only with Mr.
  Bagutti, and Mr. Artari, who did the busts
  and figures, assisted him **45 13 0**

Apr. 14th
  Paid Mr. Carpenter, statuary, in part of £25
  for figures in lead of lions sent down to
  put upon the great piers at Moulsham
  Hall **10 10 0**

22nd
  Paid John Bagley, the carpenter, for making
  the "palisadoes" for the Great Court at
  Moulsham Hall at 1s. 6d. per foot. N.B.
  I found all the stuff and paid over and
  above for turning all the columns   ...   **13 19 9**

27th
  Paid my gardener a bill for ten sacks of hay-
  seed at 18d. per sack and for 3 bushels of
  rye grass to sow the Great Court at 4s. per
  bushel, with other things **1 12 0**

May 1st
  Paid Mr. Carpenter, statuary, in further part
  and in full for his lion figures, £14, and
  for the deal cases. Total **16 0 0**

  Paid to Mr. — Dowyer, carver, in part a bill
  this day delivered in of £23 odd-money
  for carving done at Moulsham Hall in
  Essex **10 10 0**

6th
  Paid Mr. Montigny on account of a bill
  brought in of iron gates sent down to
  Moulsham Hall and set up there, on
  account **40 0 0**

17th
  Paid Mr. Mantle, plasterer, on account for
  work done at Moulsham Hall since I paid
  his great bill **15 15 0**

	£	s.	d.

May 18th

Paid Mr. Goude, stone-mason at Chelmsford, on account by bill of exchange drawn upon me by said Goude for work done at Moulsham 50 0 0

24th

Paid Mr. Vicars on account for a large quantity of yellow mohair sent down to Moulsham Hall to furnish the best apartment 100 0 0

June 1st

Paid Mr. Eves, bricklayer, in part and on account towards building the kitchen garden wall 50 0 0

26th

Paid — Roper, the lime-man, on account and in part for lime brought in for building my kitchen garden wall 40 0 0

July 1st

Paid Mrs. Hugget, the widow of — Hugget, a Maldon hoyman deceased, a bill in full for carriage of hops to London and wainscot boards from thence 3 16 6

20th

Paid Courthorpe and Eeles, timber merchants, in part of their bill given in of £199 3s. 4½d. 50 0 0

20th

Memorandum, August 20th, 1731. There has been this summer as yet but six kilns of bricks burnt for me by Spite, brickmaker.

30th

To Mr. Mason on account for painting rooms not yet measured 20 0 0

Sept 14th

Paid Dick Eves, bricklayer, in full of his bill of £94 10s. 7d., for building my kitchen

	£	s.	d.

Sept. 14th—*cont.*
garden wall, being 81 rod, with gauged work and which belongs to the gardener's house, amounts to this aforesaid sum. Paid this day in full 24 10 0

Oct. 6th
To Captain Bruce in full for 22 load of timber at 45s. per load, having paid him ten pounds, ten shillings before 38 10 0

Dec. 22nd
To Mr. Leoni in farthest part for taking care of building at Moulsham Hall 50 0 0

24th
Paid Mr. Warwick the expenses he had paid for the bringing of my fruit trees from Paris to the Port of London, which went this day to Moulsham 8 6 3

1732 Jan. 19th
Paid John Dowyer, carver, in full of all accounts 6 12 0

Feb. 17th
Paid Mr. Courthorpe and Eeles in farther part of their bill of £394 3s. 4d. given in, £50. N.B. there remains due to balance, £99 17s. wanting 1¾d. 50 0 0

29th
Paid Wm. Sullen, the sawyer, the sum of £5 3s. 6d. in full of bills delivered in to Dwinger of £11 9s. 6d., of which Dwinger had paid £6 6s. Paid now in full to this day 5 3 6

Mar. 4th
N.B. March 4th, Mr. Gainge's bill of work measured by Mr. Burningham amounts to £513 17 4

Paid Mr. Gainge on account as appears by Mr. Beard's book 411 13 0

	£	s.	d.

Mar. 4th—*cont.*

Paid more by goods bought of me by said Gainge as by said book   4   14   0

Paid more on account by Dwinger's book   55   13   0

Mar. 4th, 1731/2 paid him on account by my own hands   26   5   0

Total paid ... £498   5   0

11th

Paid Mr. Carpenter, statuary, for a medal of Seneca's head   1   11   6

April

Memorandum. Brought home from the kiln last summer for my kitchen garden wall 101,300 bricks which were burnt last summer. There is also both the kilns left full of bricks, which amounts together to 46,000. Query—how many in the kiln yard remained after the burning was over for the Summer, 1731?

7th

Paid Mr. Mason for gilding the two chimney pieces in the N.E. rooms' chief apartment   3   12   0

17th

Paid Stephen Lum, locksmith, in full of his bill of ten pounds, fourteen shillings and sixpence, the rest having been paid before   4   8   6

29th

Paid Mr. Mason in full for gilding the frame of the table in the Picture Room, and the medal, and in full for gilding to this day   1   7   0

29th

Paid Richard Eves, bricklayer, for making the drain before the Great Court of 260 foot in length, of 21 inches wide, at 6d. per

	£	s.	d.

April 29th—*cont.*

foot and also for doing the wholve in the walk and other odd jobs, and is in full of all bills and of all accounts whatever to this day inclusive 10 10 0

June 12th

Paid Dick Eves, bricklayer, for pulling down his part of the west front of Moulsham Hall, being the old building, £6 6s., and also for digging and carrying off the earth from the foundation of the kitchen there at the rate of 6d. per foot, £12 8s., the whole amounts to 18 14 0

17th

Paid Dick Eves his bill in full for day-work for digging some remaining part of the kitchen foundation, and in full of all job bills to this day inclusive 2 7 8

July 4th

Paid John Bagley, carpenter, in full for his part of taking down the west front of Moulsham Hall, as by agreement April last past 4 4 0

Aug. 23rd

Paid Mr. Mason, the painter and glazier, in full of a bill of £67 7s., and is in full of all bills given in to this day 12 16 0

25th

Paid — Roper, lime-man, on account of his bill this day delivered in for lime brought in on and since 2nd May, 1732, amounting to £29, for building my kitchen. Paid ... 15 0 0

Sept. 11th

Paid Mr. Eves, bricklayer, on account and in farther part towards building the kitchen 10 10 0

	£	s.	d.

Sept. 16th
Paid Mr. Robert Bernard, carpenter, on account for framing work for my new kitchen now building here **30   0   0**

16th
Paid Mr. Alexander Home, a gardener at Boreham, on account towards making the Great Pond in the Conduit Field, as by his receipt **20   0   0**

25th
Paid Mr. — Mason his bill for gilding the chimney piece in the drawing room, and in full of all accounts for gilding to this day **2   12   5**

Oct. 11th
Returned this day hither from London, after having been at Cambridge, and paid this morning at London to a man at Fleet Ditch for 1,000 of Dutch glazed tiles, £6, expenses in putting on board a Maldon hoy. The tiles bought of Andrew Godfrey   **6   5   0**

14th
Paid Roper, the lime-man, in full of his bill to June 25th, 1731, the sum of £19 7s. 6d., which is in full for lime for the year, 1732, the said bill amounting in all to £79 7s. 6d. and is now quite paid off, and the bill now depending, of which I have paid him £19, begins May 22nd, 1732, and is for 27 load **19   17   6**

Nov. 10th
To Spite, my brickmaker, for treading and laying on clay, five inches thick, over the offices belonging to the new kitchen, 3 days' work himself and two men, in order to be gravelled **18   0**

Nov. 11th   £   s.   d.
　　To — Baker, the blacksmith, for three iron
　　grates for three brick drains in the new
　　pond in the Conduit Field and for a grate
　　cap for the mouth of the elm trunk, and
　　for all the iron work about (*the*) sluice ...   3   3   0

　　N.B. Nov. 11th and 13th, and perhaps fol-
　　lowing days, Mr. Barnard his men were
　　endeavouring to fit the plug to the sluice
　　to the Conduit Field pond, which they had
　　done wrong at first, and consequently are
　　to mend it at their own expense.

1733　Jan. 15th
　　Paid Mr. Richard Eves, bricklayer, in
　　farther part of his bill of measured work
　　given in for the kitchen of £133 19s. 11d.,
　　having paid him before £102 10s., and
　　now, £21 more, there still remains due to
　　him but £10 9s. 8d.　　...　　...　　...   21   0   0

　　Paid Mr. Bernard, carpenter, his bill given in
　　full for framing and carpenter's work for
　　the kitchen, the passage against it and the
　　rooms over it, measured ... by Chadbourn
　　and Lum, the whole bill amounting to
　　£62 6s. 11d., paid him in part before, £30,
　　and now, £32 6s. 11d., which is in full of
　　the said bill, measured Nov. 23rd, 1732   32   6 11

Feb. 15th
　　Paid Mr. Mason, also at London, on
　　account of work done here, not yet
　　measured, but it relates to glazing and
　　plumbing about the new kitchen building,
　　with the rooms over it and the passages...   80   0   0

20th
　　Paid Dick Eves, bricklayer, on account for
　　building the south-west end of the kitchen
　　garden wall　　...　　...　　...　　...   10   10   0

	£	s.	d.

Apr. 2nd
Paid Alexander Home the sum of eight pounds ten shillings, which is in full (*for*) ten thousand clinkers by him delivered for paving the passages about my new kitchen at 17s. per 1,000   8   10   0

5th
Paid Mr. Anthony Goude, stone-mason, for paving the new kitchen with Purbeck stone etc., paid that bill in full   28   11   9

7th
Paid — Lum, the locksmith, in full for the iron bars for the new kitchen windows and for iron to the inner court for the same building, and in full of all demands ...   22   8   3

7th
Thomas Cass, the lath cleaver, in full of all accounts to this day a bill for 28 hundred of laths   12   10

7th
Paid William Fearnley, plasterer, on account   7   7   0

May 12th
Paid John Bagley, carpenter, for digging the two wells and setting up two pumps, £10 5s., the well near the house being 19 foot ½ and the other 25 foot deep, and for removing the tiled barn, £3 in all ...   13   5   0

15th
Paid Mason, plumber and glazier, in farther part of his bill delivered in of £127 17s. 4d., having paid him before, £81 4s. 9d.   25   0   0

15th
Allowed . . . to Richard Plater, paid for five weeks ending the 12th instant to the labourers in the garden, and carters, in all   19   18   2

June 17th   £   s.   d.

Paid Mr. Scheemakers, statuary, for a
statuary-marble chimney piece, with a
mask and carved egg and anchor, sent
down to Moulsham Hall for the drawing
room. Package, etc., and in full of all
accounts 28 12   0

July 13th

Paid William Banks, Quaker, for two 7-inch
brass locks for the attics over the new
kitchen at Moulsham Hall   1   1   0

30th

Paid Mr. Alexander Home in full for
making the pond in the Conduit Field and
for hedge plants, and of all accounts and
demands 24 11   6

Aug. 6th

Mr. Gainge's the joiner's men went away,
having finished the joiners' work for the
west side of this house, which I built last
year, which was the new kitchen, two
attic-rooms over it, garrets over them, and
also the passages belonging to that building.

Gave Mr. Gainge the joiner's men to drink   5   0

Memorandum, five hundred twelve-inch paving tiles will be sufficient to pave the terrace over the groining work behind the
kitchen, and sixty gutter tiles to be hollow
in the middle.

20th

August 20th, 1733, agreed with Thomas
Spite, my brickmaker, to make the above-
mentioned pantiles, and sixty gutter tiles,
which he has promised me shall be ready
in a month from this time at 7 or 8s. per
hundred.

	£	s.	d.
Aug. 22nd			
Paid Lancaster Noone, the upholsterer, his bill in full	16	9	8
Sept. 13th			
Paid Mr. Robert Bernard in full for boring 102 foot of elm pipes, 6-inch bore, for the upper pond in the Conduit Field at 8d. per foot	3	8	0
14th			
Paid Methums, brickmaker at Blackmore, his bill for rubbing-bricks at £1 5s. per 1,000	6	2	9
18th			
Paid John Barnes of Brentwood for 1,000 of pantiles, £3, and for glazed tiles, in all ...	6	3	0
Nov. 24th			
Paid Thomas Spite, brickmaker, on account of his bill delivered of £34 18s. 6d., the remaining sum due to him on the making 33,400 bricks this last summer. Paid him	5	5	0
26th			
Gave Mr. James Leoni, which he was robbed of as he came down to me on the stage coach, the 24th inst.	3	3	0
1734 Jan. 5th			
Paid Sullen, the sawyer, his two bills in full of all accounts	21	9	11
17th			
To Mr. Winter his bill in full for a stopcock and coming down to make my sluice to the pond in the Conduit Field next the house	5	10	6
29th			
Paid Mr. Eeles, timber merchant, the farther sum of twenty-five pounds on account of a bill delivered in, reduced by several payments to a balance of £84 14s. 3¾d., and now the balance due is no more than £24 19s., having paid this day	25	5	5
		(*sic*)	

	£	s.	d.

Apr. 16th
Paid Wm. Booth for the use of Mr. Cass, stone-mason, for a statuary-marble table slab sent down to Moulsham Hall, with carriage, and in full of all accounts ... — 5 10 5

29th
To Mr. Greening, nurseryman, for trees, seeds and flowers sent down to Moulsham Hall, paid him in full of a bill delivered in of £57 15s. 6d., and in full of all accounts, having paid the rest before, and now in full ... ... — 25 0 0

May 8th
Paid Wm. Banks, Quaker, his bill in full for nails, locks, tacks, ironwork, &c. ... ... — 17 9 9

27th
Paid Richard Eves, bricklayer, in full of all accounts whatever, and discharged him from my business ... ... — 42 17 11

June 4th
Paid Mr. Anthony Goude, stone-mason, his bill delivered in May 28th last past in full — 28 14 7

Paid Mr. Anthony Goude a balance due to him on Chadbourne's measuring bill, after having deducted for a yellow veined marble chimney piece taken down, and also an old bill now brought in of £2 7s. and in full of all accounts to this day ... — 10 0 0

17th
Advanced Mr. James Leoni, £25, on account of the building I am (to) go on with next year, being in distress ... ... — 25 0 0

July 31st
Paid Conquest Jones, ironmonger in Piccadilly, in full for garden nails and other nails sent down to Moulsham Hall this summer, in full to this day ... ... — 11 0 4

	£	s.	d.

Sept. 2nd

To six labourers in the garden to remove the mount to the farthest end of the garden next the stray piece, due August 31st last past. Paid this day 2 2 0

5th

Paid John Bagley, carpenter, his bill in full for the white arbour bench in the green opening in the garden 4 4 0

14th

Paid the labourers for removing the mount and carrying on the gravel walk and borders and grass verges, and continuing the elm hedge up to the place where the mount now is, viz. from north to south...   2 11 11

16th

Paid — Blatch for painting the rails at the bridge on the walk once, for painting the gate and rails by the stray piece 3 times, for painting the gate and "palisadoes" on the farther side of Ten Acres in front of the house, 3 times, for painting the arbour in the garden 3 times, and for painting the green bench under the oak in the garden once 6 15 0

28th

To the extra labourers in the garden for planting the standard elms in the principal walk and the hedge plants to the mount ...   13 5

Nov. 23rd

Paid John Middleton, bricklayer, on account of bills delivered for mending the capitals of all the piers on the front of the fore-court, and for making the drain from the vault to the water-closet to the ditch westward 5 5 0

1735 Jan. 9th   £ s. d.
      Paid Monsr. Montigny, near Hyde Park
      Corner, in full for a pair of large iron
      gates sent down to Moulsham Hall,
      £9 13s., having paid him before 40 odd
      pounds 9 13 0

      Feb. 28th
      Paid Richard Dobson of Clapham, gardener,
      for one pound of Dutch anemones,
      10s. 6d., for ½ do. English anemones,
      7s. 6d., for 50 jonquils, 2s., for 10 dozen
      double pinks, 15s., for 8 dozen of whole-
      blowing carnations, £1, for 100 polyan-
      thuses, 6s., for a box, 1s. 6d., and in full
      of all accounts 3 2 6

      March 10th
      Paid Henry Hewitt, nurseryman, his bill in
      full for 52 large standard English elms at
      3s. each, £7 16s., for 300 espalier Dutch at
      40s. per 100, £6, for 20 Dutch standard at
      18d., £1 10s., and for seeds, &c. 16 16 0

      Aug. 11th
      Advanced Mr. Leoni by the hands of John-
      son my steward the sum of £3 3s., July
      24th last past, which was forgot to be
      entered, and is on account of my new
      stables, now a-building 3 3 0

      Oct. 10th
      Paid John Bagley, carpenter, on account of
      framing the timber work for the new
      stables now building at Moulsham Hall   20 0 0

      Nov. 1st
      Paid — Chadbourne for going down and
      measuring the bricklayers', carpenters',
      joiners' and stone-masons' work of my
      new stables at Moulsham Hall, Oct. 28th
      and 29th last past 4 4 0

	£	s.	d.

Nov. 24th
Paid Thomas Spite, brickmaker, in full of all demands. N.B. The last parcel of bricks he made for me was 116,000 in the summer, 1734, and this is in full to this day, being the remainder of a bill of £40 17s.   **3 11 0**

Dec. 18th
Paid Mr. James Leoni, architect, £25, having paid him £25 before, for drawing the plan of my new stables at Moulsham Hall, and for surveying the workmen in carrying on the buildings **25 0 0**

1735 Dec. 30th
Paid John Middleton in farther part of Mr. Chadbourne's bill of the bricklayers' work, measured by himself, of the new stables, £15 3s., at one pound, four shillings per rod, being in part of said bill of £136 11s. 6½d., he having received before, £114 12s., there remains now due to him in said account, £6 16s. 6d. **15 3 0**

Paid John Bagley, carpenter, the sum of £20 in farther part of Mr. Chadbourne's bill of the carpenters' work done on the new stables amounting to £76 8s. 11½d., he having received before, £50, there now rests due, £6 8s. 11½d. **20 0 0**

1736 Jan. 1st
Paid George Gainge, joiner, in full for the workmanship and putting the two wooden cornices to my new stable here, £5 5s., having paid him before on the said account, £12 5s., in all, £17 10s. **5 5 0**

6th
Paid Baker, the farrier and blacksmith, five bills amounting to £24, being in full to the 4th Dec. last, £20 of which is for cramps and iron bolts for the new stables and the rest for shoeing my horses   ...   **24 0 0**

Feb. 5th   *£   s.   d.*

Paid to Thomas Hunt by the hands of John
Harrison a bill for £29, drawn upon me by
Mr. Anthony Goude, stone-mason at
Chelmsford, in full for the stone coping,
&c, for the new stables, at Moulsham
Hall, having paid him £21 before   ...   29   0   0

March 25th

Paid Mr. Wm. Sparkes, ironmonger, the
balance of his bill for five grates &c, of
£110, of which I had paid him £50, all or
most for Moulsham Hall, and as (*illegible*)
brought another bill of ten pound, which
I also paid, in full of all accounts   ...   70   0   0

25th

Paid Wm. Wells of Gt. Chelsea, farmer, for
carrying down to Moulsham 52 elm trees   2   2   0

Apr. 12th

Paid Elizabeth Frazer of Brompton, nursery-
woman, for 52 elm trees sent down to
Moulsham Hall, March (*should be Feb.*)
10th last past, to plant in the principal
walk in the garden   4   6   8

June 7th

Paid John Blatch of Chelmsford, plumber,
the sum of eight pounds, eighteen shillings, in full satisfaction for his bill of
£117 18s. 9d., delivered in, for sheet lead
at £1 per hundredweight for my new
stables, having paid him before at several
times the rest of his said bill, as by this
and Johnson's book and his own receipts
will appear   8   18   9

18th

Paid John Blatch of Chelmsford, plumber,
his bill in full for leaden pipes and cisterns
for my new stables at Moulsham Hall, the
pipes at 3s. per foot and cisterns at £2
each, and also for 16 hundredweight of
lead at 5 pound per foot for hipping   ...   39   4   0

	£	s.	d.

Oct. 11th

Paid Mr. John Coe of Maldon for himself and brother a bill of £190 0s. 7¼d. for fir-timber, deals, clinkers, &c for my new stables at Moulsham Hall...   ...   ...   **190   0   0**

1737   May 7th

Paid John Bagley, carpenter, in full for the framing work &c of my new stables, according to the measurement of Mr. Chadbourne, of which was left unpaid, £6 8s. 11½d., and for the racks, mangers, posts and rails in said stables, for both south and north buildings, £50 . . . and of these sums there remained unpaid, £8 9s. 2½d. which is now paid to him ...   **8   9   2½**

July 11th

Paid Mr. George Gainge, joiner, for making two dials in the front of the two stables, made of oak and "parguttee", 5 foot diameter each, with the stuff. Paid him. Unpainted **8   8   0**

27th

Paid Mr. Bishop, the Bedfordshire carpenter, the sum of twenty-six pounds, which is in full of our agreement for setting up and framing the cupolas over the new stables at Moulsham Hall, having paid him, £10, before there, in all, £36 ...   .   **26   0   0**

Sept. 17th

Paid Mr. Goude, stone-mason, on account of stone coping to the wall of the stable court and for stone caps to the piers ...   **30   0   0**

Nov. 7th

Paid Anthony Goude, stone-mason, in full of his bill of £45 for 145½ foot cubical of Portland stone at 2s. per foot, £14 11s.; and for 366 four-inches superficial circular plain work at 13d. per foot, £19 16s. 10d.

Nov. 7th—*cont.*

for 213 foot of plain at 12d. per foot, £10 13s., having paid him before as in this account 2 pages before, £30, paid him now ... 25 0 0

Dec. 9th

Paid Mr. Chadbourne, a sworn measurer from London, for measuring all John Middleton's, the bricklayer's work, and Mr. Gainge's the carpenter's and joiner's work, and all John Blatch's, the painter's and glazier's work, all which work is about the new stables, the stable court, and carthorse stable and cowhouse, and has been done since Mr. Chadbourne's ad-measurement of the new stable, Nov. 1735, all which several articles amount now to £335 1s. 4½d., and having been 3 days in measuring and one day coming down and one going up. Paid in full. N.B. everything is now measured about the stables 5 5 0

1738 Jan. 28th

Paid Mr. Bradley, clockmaker, by the hands of his son, in part of his bill of £92 0s. 3d. for the stable clock put up at Moulsham Hall, £55, for painting and drawing the sundial plate and the clock-dial plate, with the gnomon to the sundial, £11 8s., for a large bell, for the clock, weight, 1 cwt. 3 qrs., 21, at 15d. per pound, £13 11s. 3d., with some other small things, besides two weathercocks of copper, with iron work and painting and gilding, £10, in all £92 0s. 3d., paid on account, £80, because the sundial is not set true, and some other things want to (*be*) rectified 80 0 0

Feb. 9th

To Mr. James Leoni for going down to Moulsham and drawing for me a little plan for the boundary of my garden, and some other little things 10 10 0

	£	s.	d.

Feb. 16th
Paid Mr. Leoni for a little horizontal sundial, made at Paris by one Butterfield, an Englishman, with needles, which he bought for me 1 1 0

Apr. 8th
Paid John Middleton, the bricklayer, for turning the brick arch of the wholve in the walk, for turning a brick arch near the white rails to the park ponds, for 2 brick arches going into the field at the upper end of the stray piece and one other into the ditch to the garden southward near the mount, and for some other small drains 3 16 6

June 3rd
Paid Edmond Bolton, nurseryman at Ilford, for 40 standard elms and 300 hedge-elm plants for the new walk 9 5 3
(sic)

N.B. The elm hedge plants for the farthest new long walk to the Perry Field cost £2 5s. per hundred, and 40 standard elms at £6 per 100, cost £2 8s.

Sept. 11th
Paid John Banks for a fine wood stock lock, 3s. 6d., for one pair of hinges, 3s., for a staple, 8d., for 1 key, 1s. 6d., all for the new dogs' kennel, and for 1 *(blank)* of iron hoops for small beer hogsheads, £1 5s.   1 13 8

Oct. 21st
Paid Thomas Chadbourne, admeasurer, for . . . measuring . . . the wall in the ha-ha, and also the wall and piers at the end of said wall westward, also my dog kennel and also 2 rooms added to the gardener's house in the garden 5 5 0

	£	s.	d.

1739 Apr. 3rd
Go down to Moulsham Hall this day with my Lady Fitzwalter and carry with us Mr. Leoni in order to mark out the foundation for a new brewhouse and dairy.

July 16th
Began to lay the foundation of my new dairy, wash-house and laundry.

Aug. 4th
Paid David Jefferies his bill in full for carting 29,000 bricks from the kiln in Galleywood Common at 3s. 6d. per 1,000, towards the new dairy and new laundry... **5 6 6**

Sept. 26th
Paid a bill drawn upon me by Madame Wolters at Rotterdam for 2,175 white Dutch tiles for my new dairy at Moulsham Hall **6 19 0**

Oct. 16th
Paid Mr. Thomas Heath, mathematical instrument maker, for a brass horizontal dial plate now set up in the court before the house at Moulsham Hall, 20 inches diameter. Paid him £12 12s., and for a box, 5s., in full of all accounts **12 17 0**

Nov. 12th
Paid John Blatch, plumber, painter and glazier, on account and in part of his bill of £61 12s. 2d., this day delivered in for lead and inside and outside work about the new brewhouse, laundry and dairy the sum of **30 0 0**

1740 May 28th
Paid — Carter, stone-mason for the pedestal for the dial plate set up at Moulsham Hall, 1739, in full **8 0 0**

	£	s.	d.

July 5th
 Paid Mr. Gainge for making a seat for the
 garden, now painted white, 13s., and for
 making a framed stand for the gardener to
 clip the garden hedges with, 16s. 3d. ...   1 9 3

26th
 Paid Stephen Lum, locksmith, in full of his
 bill of £18 17s. 6d.... ... ...   8 6 0

Sept. 18th
 Paid Mr. Chadbourne for coming hither and
 measuring the work of G. Gainge, carpenter, in my new dairy, wash house and
 laundry, and all the carpenter's work in
 the poultry yard and all the bricklayer's
 work not before measured about the said
 poultry yard, and also all his work in
 building my new pigeon house, and the
 painting of all the flights of rails in the
 Great Court before the house, and the
 new white-painting of my dressing room,
 and the paving before the dairy, poultry
 yard and laundry, with other small things,
 in full 4 4 0

Oct. 8th
 Paid Mr. Goude, stone-mason, Mr. Chadbourne's bill of admeasurement, 17th of
 inst. Sept. for squaring and laying the
 Newcastle stone before the dairy and
 laundry at 2d. per foot &c, in full ...   6 8 6

1741 Apr. 3rd
 Paid Edward Bolton, nurseryman at Ilford,
 for plants for that part of the plantation in
 my garden next the mount, and in full.
 Planted in Oct. last 9 5 8

1743 May 8th
 Go this day to Moulsham to see the foundation laid for the North front, laid in order
 to the finishing of the whole building, Mr.
 Leoni having been there ever since the 5th
 inst. May.

		£	s.	d.
1744	Jan. 17th			
	Paid Isaac Eeles, timber merchant, on account on his bill of timber sent down to Moulsham Hall of £122 7s. 4d.	62	7	0
	July 10th			
	Paid Mr. James Leoni the sum of £15 10s., which with £84 10s. which he has received from me since May 4th, 1743, makes the complete sum of £100 and is in full to the 4th of May, 1744, for surveying my new building at Moulsham Hall. N.B. This agreement is not to continue for the current year, being determined not to give him more than £50	15	10	0
	Nov. 29th			
	Paid Wm. Cooley, stone-mason, on account for work he has done at Moulsham Hall	30	0	0
1745	Apr. 6th			
	Paid Mr. Robert Dawson for work now doing at Moulsham Hall the farther sum of £30 on account, Johnson, my steward, having paid him before for plasterer's work, £54 13s. 6d., so that there rests now due to him £48 2s. 9½d.	30	0	0
	Oct. 19th			
	G. Murray, carver, on account of his bill of £54 5s. 8½d.	25	0	0
1746	Feb. 4th			
	Paid Thomas Stevens, locksmith, on account of a bill delivered in of £46 15s. 2d. ...	20	0	0
	Mar. 20th			
	Paid Mr. Richards, carver, on account of a bill delivered in for carving work done at Moulsham Hall, £106 19s. 5d.	50	0	0
	Apr. 29th			
	Paid Mrs. Artari by virtue of a letter of attorney from her husband, Joseph Artari, *stuccatore*, the sum of £21 15s. having paid her £5 5s. before with what I had			

		£	s.	d.

Apr. 29th—*cont.*
paid before that to her said husband, is in full for doing the ceiling in my Great Room at Moulsham Hall, and of all accounts **21 15 0**

June 8th
Mr. Leoni, my Italian architect, died this day. Sent him during his illness, which lasted about one month, *par charité*   ...   **8 8 0**

1747 Dec. 14th
Paid Thomas Carter, stone-mason, the farther sum of fifty pounds for the marble statuary chimney piece in my Great Room at Moulsham Hall. Bill £201 0s. 11d., Paid £150. Rests still due   ...   **50 0 0**

1748 Feb. 1st
Paid Robert Parsons, stone carver at Bath, for four pair of vases sent down to Moulsham Hall **16 4 0**

3rd
Paid Levy Perry of Brooke's wharf for wharfage and housing and carriage of 4 pairs of stone vases from Bath to London   **7 4 11**

1749 Feb. 10th
Paid John Cheere for 8 "bustos" and casing sent to Moulsham Hall, 1743   ...   ...   **5 1 0**

CHAPTER THREE

RUNNING THE HOUSEHOLD

(a) *The Pall Mall house: its overheads, maintenance, household supplies and equipment*

In the accounts Fitzwalter frequently writes of "my house in the Pall Mall", but never refers to it as Schomberg House, the name by which it came to be known. It was really his wife's: her father, Meinhardt, Duke of Schomberg, leased it from the Crown in 1694 and reconstructed it *c.* 1698, in those few years which probably formed the best period in town-house architecture—William-with-out-Mary. Schomberg died in 1719; his elder daughter, Frederica, lived on at Schomberg House with her first husband, the Earl of Holderness, and then with her second husband, Fitzwalter. It was divided into 3 dwellings in 1769, and Gainsborough lived in one of them. The façade of one dwelling was brutally remodelled in 1850. In 1956 the Crown sold the lease on condition that the façade was retained. The house was then demolished and an office block was built; the Victorian eastern third of the façade was restored to match the remainder, "an act of belated justice", as Peterborough called it in the *Daily Telegraph*.

In Fitzwalter's time, well before its division into three, it was a most commodious house, with 33 tall windows (perhaps more) looking down on Pall Mall. He would probably have regarded Moulsham Hall, which he rebuilt with loving care, as his principal home, but the fact is that he spent far more time in the town house. Between 1733 and 1746 he occupied it on an average on as many as 238 days a year, and even in his wife's last years, 1746–51, when long visits to Bath and Tunbridge Wells became more frequent, he was there for 179 days on an annual average.

It was costly to run and maintain. There were the overheads. The Crown rent was fixed at £40 per annum, land tax varied from £18 to £43 10s. and the poor rate from £16 5s. to £25. Some overheads increased with the years: the window tax went up from £1 10s. to a level around 5 guineas; the payments to the parish watch and beadles increased from £1 14s. to £5 and to the parish scavengers from £1 15s. to £3 15s. The water rent went down from £6 to £5 in 1743, and in 1749 Fitzwalter secured a new fire insurance policy at a premium of £4 10s. on £3,000, instead of the earlier £6. His annual contribution to the watering of the street remained steady at one guinea.

Over the years 1742–52, at least 33 craftsmen and their firms were concerned with the maintenance of the house. Unfortunately, the full cost of their services will never be known; some of the bills were rendered at irregular intervals without specifying the time they covered; Fitzwalter sometimes forgot to enter them; and there is always that missing account-book. There were those jobs liable to occur frequently and calling for the services of the Webb family, the carpenters, of Furness the brazier and Corner the glazier. There were the infrequent little jobs: various ironmongers putting in small grates for about £2 apiece; Richard Lankeshaw providing two new lamps for the street door; Montagu painting the iron rails on the street side at 5d. per yard; John Mears emptying the water closet vault about every third year for £7 5s. There were larger undertakings: Thomas Dacres paved the part of the street in front of the house for 16 guineas; Thomas Ayling laid a new stone terrace in the garden; Pickford the mason fixed a chimney piece of marble in the dining room; Robert Dawson, plasterer, made two stucco cornices and two new ceilings for £31 11s. In 1740, Mrs. Webb's men carried out "all the carpenters' work done at the top of my house in Pall Mall in order to its being new leaded"; Cock, the plumber, did the leading and Evan Thomas the slating; and the total cost was £175.

The house had to be kept supplied. Coal was an expensive item, about £189–£220 a year; the oil bills were probably about one-tenth of that sum. Dominic Warren of Pall Mall supplied most of the glasses and some of the china for the house and for Moulsham Hall; but from time to time Lady Fitzwalter would buy china at other shops, and one consignment of Dresden china was imported. Mr. Arne, father of the composer of "Rule Britannia", supplied "grey furniture for mourning on the death of my Lady Dowager Fitzwalter", Fitzwalter's mother. Other payments are given in other sections of this chapter; even so, a complete analysis of the running

SCHOMBERG HOUSE, PALL MALL

of the Pall Mall house is impossible—so much of this is caught up in the household bills paid by Lady Fitzwalter and only the totals of these are generally given. Incidentally, even less is known about the running of Moulsham Hall, and the Fitzwalters' first country house, Popes in Hertfordshire; this was mainly the responsibility of the steward.

Fortunately, rather more is known about one essential part of Fitzwalter's household equipment, his silver. Usually, it was kept at Schomberg House in the custody of the butler, but some of it travelled to and fro with the family or with Mears, the carrier, between Pall Mall and Moulsham Hall. Six silversmiths' names are given in the accounts, but the total spent on five of them is insignificant compared with Fitzwalter's patronage of the sixth, the incomparable Paul de Lamerie.

The evidence for Fitzwalter's transactions with de Lamerie consists of a dozen account book entries, three long bills (D/DM F13) and an inventory of Fitzwalter's plate. The book entries merely record payments on account to de Lamerie. The three bills appear to be the 2nd, 3rd and 4th of four accounts presented to Fitzwalter between c. 1725 and 1738. They are difficult to interpret: it seems that bills 1 (missing), 2 and 3 overlap, and possibly, bill 4, too; this makes it hard to determine exactly how much Fitzwalter ordered from de Lamerie. Possibly the total to 1743 may be £2,146 2s. 11d.; direct payments by Fitzwalter on account to 1752 and allowances on old silver appear to total another £2,115 4s. The second of the surviving bills is reproduced here. The inventory of Fitzwalter's plate at Schomberg House (D/DM F12, not reproduced here) was taken on June 22nd, 1739, by Henry Longmore, butler, and witnessed by William Wilkins (Fitzwalter's valet), Maurice (*alias* Mansell) Roberts (his cook) and Henry Hebert, silversmith. It shows a total of 4,684 oz. 19 dwt., plus 44 knives, 12 dessert forks and 2 odd spoons. Four or five of the items can be identified as being by de Lamerie; a closer examination by experts might lead to the identification of more pieces. As an example of price, an oval tureen weighing 204 oz. 5 dwt. cost £62 19s. 6d. for the silver, £25 10s. for making and £1 for engraving, a total of £89 9s. 6d.

References

The substance of the first paragraph is derived from *The Survey of London,* xxix, pp. 368-77.

The Pall Mall House—selective extracts

		£	s	d.
1725	Jan. 29th			
	To Mr. Peres (*?Edward Pearce*) silversmith in full of all accounts	20	6	6
	Aug. 17th			
	To Mr. Samuel Horseley, coal merchant, in part of a bill of £209 9s. 6d., paid £100. The 40 chaldron of coals laid in this present August, not being on this bill ...	100	0	0
	Oct. 7th			
	To a woman for lighting the lamps ...	4	0	0
1726	May 2nd			
	To Mr. Lamerie, silversmith, in farther part of his bill for plate	100	0	0
	16th			
	To a spying-glass for Lady Holderness ...		10	6
	Oct. 29th			
	For a brass lock for the bedchamber door	1	1	0
	30th			
	Paid Mr. Arne in full for grey furniture for mourning on the death of my Lady Dowager Fitzwalter	30	0	0
	Nov. 15th			
	To 30 yds. of fine huckaback at 3s. 6d. per yd. to Mr. R. Gale	5	5	0
1727	May 12th			
	To Mr. Blun for a grate for my Lady Holderness's dressing-room, with tongs and fire shovel	2	10	0
	Dec. 20th			
	To—Dissel, the plumber, in full of a bill long since given in of £43, having before paid £25, pay the remaining £18 ...	18	0	0
1728	May 3rd			
	Paid to the Chelsea water one year and half a quarter due Lady Day last past, and from that time laid in the Hyde Park water at £6 per annum	4	10	0

		£	s.	d.
1729 Mar. 25th To Mr. White, silversmith and excise officer, a bill for plate, £14 14s. on my brother Fitzwalter's account		17	8	0
June 23rd Friday 20th and Monday 23rd were sent in 28 chaldrons of coals to fill the two vaults in Pall Mall, by John Davis. Not paid, at 30s. per chaldron		57	0	0
Sept. 1st Agreed with Benjamin Boswell of Westminster, gardener, to keep my garden in the Pall Mall from Michaelmas next for one year at 2 guineas per year.				
Dec. 17th To Mr. Sparkes for a circular grate for the drawing-room in Pall Mall		3	10	0
1730 Jan. 28th Paid water rent for Hyde Park water to Christmas 1729 in full for one year ...		6	0	0
Feb. 2nd To Grubb and partner the half year due for the poor's rate at Christmas last ...		8	15	0
9th To the beadle for 4 quarters for the watch for St. James's parish to Christmas last ...		1	14	0
Mar. 10th To Mr. Stallard, bricklayer, his bill in full for work done in the Pall House (*sic*) amounting, £11 7s. 8d., and the bill he paid for slating 14s. 3d., in all		12	1	11
Apr. 17th To the land tax for my house in the Pall Mall for the year, 1729, £32 12s. 6d. N.B., the year before it was but £29, but, this last year they had a reassessment of 3d. per pound which increased it so much, but this year is reduced from 3s. in the pound to 2s.		32	12	6

	£	s.	d.
May 5th			
Paid the window tax due Lady Day last for the house in the Pall Mall	1	10	0
Aug. 13th			
To Mr. Anderson, brazier, for a copper thing with a division for knives, forks and spoons	1	5	0
Oct. 7th			
Paid for the watering the streets last summer	1	1	0
12th			
Paid ... to B. Boswell for carrying and laying 19 load of gravel in my garden ...	1	11	6
Dec. 14th			
Paid the glazier's bill in full for cleaning and mending the windows in the house in Pall Mall	3	5	6
1731 Apr. 10th			
Paid the land tax for the house in Pall Mall, being four quarterly payments due Lady Day last at 2s. per pound, amounting to	18	3	0
May 18th			
Paid a bill to Mr. Anderson and Sparkes, braziers, for a copper cistern for ten bottles, £3 5s., for a deep copper basket for plates, £2 5s., for a partition basket for knives, £1 7s. 6d.	6	17	6
Dec. 20th			
Allowed also a bill paid to said Thomas Ayling in full of all accounts, except £1, for laying my stone terrace entirely, a good deal of the stone being new, at my house in the Pall Mall	4	8	5
1732 Jan. 6th			
Paid Mr. Mantle in full for whitewashing and plasterer's work in the Pall Mall ...	4	8	5
Apr. 24th			
To Mr. John Perkins, coal merchant, in part of a bill delivered in of £114 7s. 2d. ...	50	0	0

		£	s.	d.
June 2nd				
Paid to the new great sewer in the Pall as taxed by the Commissioner at 2s. 2d. per pound of £290 per annum, rent		31	8	4
To my Lady Fitzwalter for a dozen soup china plates		1	10	0
July 12th				
Paid Mr. Boson, carver, for carving the chimney piece which is gilt in the dining room here, and in full		5	12	0
Aug. 12th				
Paid Mr. Burton, oil man, his bill and in full of all accounts to the 29th of July last past		9	0	7½
Nov. 18th				
Paid—Walker, tin-man, for two street lamps and seven house lamps, and in full		1	17	0
1733 Mar. 16th				
Paid at the Royal Exchange Assurance Office in the City for a policy of assurance of £3,000 on the house in Pall Mall in case of accident by fire. Paid by Johnson, my butler		6	0	0
Sept. 6th				
Paid Edward Dacres for an entire paving of the street before my door in the Pall Mall, June, 1733		16	16	0
1734 Jan. 11th				
Paid Dominic Warren a bill for glasses sent down to Moulsham in June last		5	6	0
Paid to do. a bill for glasses bought today, and in full		1	1	0
19th				
Paid—Perkins, coal merchant, his bill in full of all accounts, having discharged him some time since		129	15	2
Mar 5th				
For a silver milk jug		4	4	0

		£	s.	d.

June 13th
Paid Mears for emptying the vault in the house in the Pall and taking out 29 ton of soil, having emptied it 3 year and ½ before and took just the same quantity, at 5s. per ton, comes to 7 5 0

1735 Feb. 10th
Paid John Hutton of Paul's Churchyard for a set of gilt leather hangings, blue and gold, with a damask figure and mosaic border, for the room next the street at the head of the great stairs in the house in Pall Mall 22 0 0

Dec. 16th
To Corner, glazier, his bill in full 3 13 5½

1736 Jan. 6th
To my Lady Fitzwalter for a silver soup spoon bought at Chelmsford 2 2 0

Nov. 10th
To Miles Shutcliff, coal merchant, in part of his bill delivered in the 4th inst. of £87 11s. 6d., paid £50, so that there now rests due on said bill, £37 11s. 6d. 50 0 0

1737 June 27th
Paid for water glasses and drinking glasses and decanters for one year and 3 quarters, the bill in full of Dominic Warren, glassman, Pall Mall 7 19 6

1738 Jan. 6th
Paid Joseph Gillet, a Quaker, cutler in St. James's Market, for 2 cases, each of one dozen knives, forks and spoons, £3, and for one case of dessert knives, forks and spoons, £1 12s. and for blades of knives, oyster knives &ca, in all and in full ... 6 0 5

30th
Paid Mr. Neville, silversmith, near St. James's Markets in Norris Street, the difference between six salvers or hand-

	£	s.	d.

Jan. 30th—*cont.*

waiters, which he had of me, and the six
I had in exchange fashion, and my coat
of arms included. Paid him the difference
and in full of all accounts 7 12 0

May 11th

Paid Edward (*surname omitted*), silversmith in Lombard Street, for 14 tickets,
silver, for wine bottles, at 5s. 6d. each ...   3 17 0

Nov. 4th

Paid the Earl of Ancram for my case of
pistols, mounted with silver and made for
the Duke of Douglas by order of Captain
Wilson, and paid for by him to — the
gunsmith, which my Lord Ancram, when
last in London, paid the said Captain
Wilson on my account. Paid my lord in
full for said pistols 9 11 0

1739 Feb. 8th

Paid Robert Jupp and Charles Bush, over-
seers of the poor of the parish of St.
James's, 4 quarters due at Christmas last
for my house in the Pall Mall, rated at
£300 per annum 17 10 0

24th

Paid Mr. Pickford, stonemason by Hyde
Park Corner, for a chimney piece of
statuary marble in the drawing-room
above stairs in the house in the Pall Mall,
put up in December 1738. Paid him now
for said chimney piece, £18 0s. 10d., and
for some other small jobs, and in full of
all accounts, £6, in all 24 0 10

27th

Paid six quarters due the 2nd of December
last for the watch and beadles of the
parish of St. James's. When the book was
first brought to me, my house was rated
at £400 per annum, upon which I refused

	£	s.	d.
Feb. 27th—*cont.*			
to pay till it was lowered to £300 per annum. The beadle then carried the book to the clerk of the vestry, who did lower it to £300 per annum, and brought it, so lowered, next day, upon which I paid then	5	6	3
Apr. 10th			
Paid H. Stallwood, my bricklayer, his bill in full for measured work by Mr. Thomas Chadbourne, £3 8s., and also his bill of jobbing work in full of all jobbing-work, £6 3s. N.B. pointing and rubbing the front of the house in Pall Mall not yet paid for. He agreed with me to do it for 12 guineas; however, I design to give him 15 guineas	9	11	0
June 22nd			
Paid Charles Vere, china-man in Fleet Street, for a hexagon china soup dish, £2 2s., for 12 hexagon, also blue and white, soup plates, 4s. each, £2 8s., six blue and white handle chocolate cups, with ten dishes and saucers, blue and white, and in full	6	3	0
Sept. 26th			
Paid Mr. Sidwick his and the housekeeper's fees at the Jewel Office for the 1000 ounces of silver plate allowed me by the King as Treasurer of his Household ...	4	9	0
Oct. 3rd			
Paid H. Stallwood, bricklayer, for cleaning and pointing the front of my house in Pall Mall in the summer, 1739, and in full of all accounts	15	15	0
6th			
Paid Hebert, silversmith, for two silver ladles for the tureens, &ca and in full ...	9	19	6

		£	s.	d.

Dec. 11th
Paid — Hebert, silversmith, for a silver standish, weight about 50 ounces at 2s. 6d. per ounce, fashion, of which allowed at the Jewel Office, 32 ounces, and for what is over and above I now pay said Hebert, £8 8s., in full of all accounts 8 8 0

1740 Mar. 6th
Paid Mr. Richards, carver in wood, for carving the chimney piece in (the) drawing room above stairs in the Pall Mall house, and in full of all accounts ... 12 2 0

Apr. 3rd
Paid Benjamin Griffin, gunsmith, for cleaning and repairing nine cases of pistols, the steel-mounted at 2s. per pair and the brass-mounted at 1s. 6d. per pair, in full and in the whole 1 9 6

Oct. 31st
Paid Mears "cartaker", for carrying my plate to Moulsham 2 0 0

Nov. 19th
Paid Richard Lankeshaw for two new lamps for the street door 1 11 6

Dec. 22nd
Paid my house porter his bill in full for expenses for a box of Dresden china from the custom house, £0 19s. 19 0

1741 Jan. 17th
Paid Mrs. Elizabeth Webb her bill for all the carpenters' work done on the top of my house in Pall Mall in order of its being new leaded, as it was last summer, 1740 ... ... 21 8 1½

Paid Evan Thomas his bill for slating my house in Pall Mall last summer, 1740, in full of all accounts 20 2 8

		£	s.	d.

Jan. 28th

Paid Mr. Cock, plumber, in farther part of his bill of £133 9s. 8d., the sum of fifty pounds, so now there rests due to him only £33 9s. 8d.   50   0   0

Apr. 7th

Paid John Watson and John Durson collectors for the land tax at 4s. per pound for my house in Pall Mall for the year, 1740. The rent of my house last year set at £161. The year before it was set at £146 *per (annum)*   32   4   0

Nov. 1st

Paid Montagu for painting twice over the iron rails on the street side, at 5d. per yard, and in full   1   15   0

1742   July 19th

To Furness, the brazier, his bill in full to Feb. 6th, 1741/2   15   6   5

1742   Nov. 27th

Paid Mr. Thomas Carter, stonemason, for a large black and white cistern for bottles, £21, and for other jobs, £6, and in full of all accounts   28   0   0
            (sic)

Dec. 9th

Paid Robert Dawson, plasterer, for making 2 stucco cornices above stairs and 2 new-floated ceilings in the said rooms, and whitewashing many places of my house in Pall Mall, and in full of all accounts ...   31   11   0

1743   Jan. 14th

Paid my water rent for one whole year due at Christmas, 1742, to the proprietors of the waterworks at London Bridge, and in full   5   0   0

		£	s	d.
Jan. 24th				
Paid Mr. Chenevix for a silver sugar caster, weight 17 oz. 16., at 6s. 2d. per oz. and fashion at 3s. per oz., with other small things, and in full of all accounts ...		9	11	3
31st				
Paid John Taylor, china-man, his bill for a set of china dishes sent down to Moulsham Hall, and in full of all accounts ...		16	3	6
1744	Mar. 22nd			
	Paid my Lady Fitzwalter for 6 cups and saucers and milk jug of white Dresden china	3	3	0
1745	Mar. 22nd			
	Paid Charles Hill for a silver orange-strainer, and in full	1	9	0
	Apr. 22nd			
	Paid Henry Parsons for one dozen of huckaback towels	1	15	0
	25th			
	Paid Mrs. Corner, the widow and administratrix of my glazier, deceased, her bill in full	14	14	0
	May 4th			
	Paid Mrs. Godfrey, silversmith, for a large, silver milk jug	2	0	0
1746	Feb. 24th			
	Paid Becket, sword-cutler, in full for cleaning the arms in my hall		10	0
	25th			
	Paid Griffin, gunsmith, in full for cleaning the arms in my hall	2	1	0
	June 28th			
	Paid Mrs. Anne Shutcliff, widow, on account of a bill delivered in for costs of £81 18s. due to her husband, lately deceased, £40. Rests still due in said bill, £41 8s. ...	40	0	0

	£	s	d.

July 3rd

Paid Mr. Paddey, Receiver of the Crown rents, for the parish of St. James's Westminster, two years' rent due and in full to Michaelmas, 1745, land tax already paid, pay now, £80   80   0   0

30th

Paid Mr. Carter, stonemason, his bill in full for a statuary chimneypiece for the northwest dressing room, and for one of veined marble for the west bedchamber, both below stairs   44   15   10

1747 Feb. 16th

Wheatley, the glazier, his bill in full ...   2   16   0

June 20th

Paid Mr. John Le Sage for a silver standish for my Lady Fitzwalter   5   12   6

Dec. 7th

Paid Ross, coal merchant, on account of a bill of £67 6s. 4d.   25   0   0

1748 Jan. 11th

Paid for a half-pint silver mug for my Lady Fitzwalter to drink her asses' milk in ...   1   13   0

Oct. 5th

Paid John Mears, "cartaker", for emptying the water closet   7   5   0

1749 Apr. 19th

Paid — tin-man, for the kitchen, his bill in full   15   0

1750 Jan. 29th

Paid Mr. Stephens for an iron knocker for my street door   5   0

Nov. 2nd

Paid Mr. Torbet for a steel-cut fender at 8s. 6d. per foot, &ca   2   3   4

		£	s	d.
1752	**Mar. 23rd**			
	Paid — Wagg for a new kitchen jack, and in full	10	10	0
	Apr. 3rd			
	Paid for the window lights, Pall Mall ...	5	6	0
	10th			
	Paid the executors of Mr. Paul de Lamerie, silversmith, in full of all accounts due to the deceased	40	15	3
	Dec. 14th			
	Paid Stafford, pewterer, his bill in full ...	12	12	4
1753	**May 11th**			
	Paid the turner's bill in full	8	4	6
	June 21st			
	Paid — Pearson for stoneware plates and dishes	9	4	0
1754	**Aug. 30th**			
	Paid — Ross, coal merchant, in full of all demands, and turned him off	85	7	11
	Sept. 5th			
	Paid John Chips, my town gardener, his bill in full for one year for taking care of my garden here	2	14	6
	Oct. 31st			
	Paid Michael Morton his bills for charcoal and sea coal, and in full of all demands ...	39	3	10
	Dec. 4th			
	Paid Thomas Bromwich for paper-hangings &ca, and in full of all demands	5	14	8

The Pall Mall House   A bill from Paul de Lamerie, 1736

(*page* 1)	£	*s.*	*d.*
To 12 knives, 12 spoons, 12 forks, 47 oz. 3 dwt., 6s. 2d. per oz.	14	10	8
Fashion of the knives, 6s. per piece ...	3	12	0
Fashion of the spoons & forks, 2s. 6d. per piece	3	0	0
Blades	1	0	0
Engraving		18	0
Case for them all	1	10	0
2 salvers, 30 oz. 5 dwt. at 6s. 2d. per oz. ...	9	6	6
Fashion, 12d. per oz.	1	10	0
Engraving		15	0
Altering the 2 salvers, silver and making ...	1	15	0
To 4 candlesticks, snuffer & pan, 69 oz. 14 dwt. at 6s. 2d. per oz.	21	10	0
Fashion, 2s. 6d. per oz.	8	15	0
Engraving		15	0
To a coffee pot, 35 oz. 15 dwt. at 6s. 2d. per oz.	11	0	6
Fashion, 2s. per oz.	3	12	0
Handle		3	0
Engraving		7	6
To an oval dish, 92 oz. 13 dwt. at 6s. 2d. oz.	28	9	8
Fashion, 2s. per oz.	9	4	0
Engraving		2	0
To 12 dishes & 3 dozen plates, 1260 oz. 15 dwt. at 6s. 2d. per oz.	388	14	6
Fashion, 18d. per oz.	94	10	0
Engraving, 3s. per piece	7	4	0
Carried over ...	612	4	4

				£	s.	d.
(page 2)						
		Brought over	...	612	4	4
To an oval tureen, 204 oz. 5 dwt., 6s. 2d. per oz.	...	...	... ...	62	19	6
Fashion, 2s. 6d. per oz.	...	...	...	25	10	0
Engraving	... ...	...	... ...	1	0	0
To 4 candlesticks, French	...	...	...	5	5	0
A large salver, 71 oz. at 6s. 2d. (*per oz.*)	...			21	17	10
Fashion, 18d. per oz.		...	... ...	5	6	6
Engraving	...	... ...	... ...	1	1	0
To plate brushes and skins	...	...	...	1	0	0
Engraving a water pot	...	...	...		6	0
To 2 spoons 4 oz. 19 dwt. at 6s. 2d. per oz.				1	10	7
Fashion, 2s. 6d. per piece	...	...	...		5	0
Engraving	...	...	... ...		3	0
To 3 blades	...	...	... ...	...		4	6
To a soup ladle, 8 oz. 2 dwt. at 6s. 2.(*d*)	...			2	19	11
Fashion, 2s. per oz.	...	...	... ...		16	0
Engraving	...	...	... ...		1	6
To 8 skewers, 6 oz. 10 dwt. at 6s. per oz.	...			1	19	0
Fashion, 3s. per piece	...	...	...	1	14	0
To a new handle to a large coffee pot		...		3	0
To mending a spoon	...	...	...		1	0
To mending a salver foot	...	...	...		1	6
To a skin for plate	...	...	...	...		2	6
		Carried up	...	745	11	2

		£	s.	d.
(*page* 3)				
	Brought up ...	745	11	2
	To a ring with 4 branches, 4 buttons, 4 round saucers & a large basin, 158 oz. 8 dwt. at 6s. 3d. per oz.	49	10	0
	Fashion, 3s. per oz.	23	15	6
	Engraving the 4 round saucers & the large basin all with ornaments & the 4 arms ...	5	5	0
1728	May 11th			
	Tea ring, 37 oz. 11 dwt. at 6s. 3d.	11	14	8
	Fashion, 3s. per oz.	5	12	6
	Sept. 26th			
	To 2 brushes for plate		4	0
1729	Feb. 27th			
	To 2 broad brushes for plate		6	0
	Mar. 14th			
	To mending the screw of a branch saucer		2	0
1730	Dec. 3rd			
	To mending the screw of a saucer		2	0
1731	Apr. 1st			
	To engraving the coronet on 3 dozen of knurled plates at 9d. per piece	1	7	0
	13th			
	To 3 dishes with knurls, 147 oz. at 6s. 2½d. per oz.	45	12	7
	Fashion, 18d. per oz.	11	0	6
	Engraving		15	0
1731	July 12th			
	To 4 large candlesticks, 88 oz. 12 dwt. at 6s. 2½(d)	27	10	0
	Fashion, 2s. per oz.	8	17	0
	To mending a spoon		1	0
1732	Feb. 16th			
	To 2 broad plate brushes and 2 skins ...		10	0
	To a knurled soup dish, 78 oz. 4 dwt. at 6s. 1d. per oz.	23	15	8
	Fashion, 18d. per oz.	5	17	0
	Engraving		5	0
1732/3	Feb. 3rd			
	To a lamp, 8 oz. 13 dwt. at 6s. per oz. ...	2	11	10
	Fashion, 2s. per oz.		17	0
	21st			
	To a new handle to a tea kettle		1	6
	Carried over ...	971	3	11

		£	s.	d.
(page 4)				
Brought over ...		971	3	11
1733	May 22nd			
	To a large kitchen spoon, 3 oz. 10 dwt. at			
	6s. per oz.	1	1	0
	Fashion		7	6
	Engraving the crest and coronet		1	6
	To a new handle to a large coffee pot or			
	decanter		3	0
1734	July 19th			
	To mending 2 forks, adding 6 new prongs			
	to them; they belonging to a travelling			
	case		4	0
	To a case for the travelling equipage ...		15	0
	Oct. 25th			
	To mending a spoon		1	0
1735	Nov. 6th			
	To mending, with new boiling and burnish-			
	ing, a shaving basin, water pot and wash-			
	ball box, with silver added to the water			
	pot	1	0	0
	To mending and fitting up a tureen ...		7	6
1736	Feb. 4th			
	To mending a water pot		4	0
	Apr. 8th			
	To engraving a ladle		2	0
	To mending a dessert spoon		1	0
	14th			
	To mending the screw of a branch saucer		2	0
		975	13	5
		871	0	5
	Remain	104	13	0

	£	s.	d.
(*page* 5)			
Received old silver, 78 oz. at 5s. 2d. per oz.	20	5	3
Received a chocolate pot, teakettle & chafing dish, 116 oz. 15 dwt. at 5s. 2d. per oz.	30	3	1
Received at several times & given receipts for the same	600	0	0
1728 Dec. 31st			
Received and given a note	50	0	0
Received an old dish 80 oz. 3 dwt. at 5s. 3d. per oz.	21	0	9
(1729) Jan. 2nd			
Received a monteith, 70 oz. 8 dwt. at 5s. 3d. per oz.	19	10	6
Received a parcel of several pieces, 48 oz. 15 dwt. at 5s. per oz.	12	3	9
Received some small pieces, 2 oz. 15 dwt. at 5s. per oz.		13	9
Received gold ring, 1 oz. 16 dwt. at £3 10s. per oz.	6	6	0
1730/31			
Feb. 18th			
Received	50	0	0
Mar. 8th			
Received an old lamp, 5 oz. 6 dwt. at 5s. 3d. per oz.	1	7	0
13th			
Received six sconces, 225 oz. & an old spoon 1 oz. 12 dwt. at 5s. 3d.	59	9	6
	871	0	5

(*Then, in Fitzwalter's hand*)

May 15th, 1735, rec'd. of the Right Hon. the Earl Fitzwalter the sum of fifty pounds on account	£50	0	0

(*signed by de Lamerie*)   Paul de Lamerie.

(b) *Food and Drink*

Food

In the Fitzwalter household, food was plentiful and cheap. Henry Shuttleworth, the Great Baddow butcher, who bought lambs from the home farm at Moulsham Hall, supplied the household with beef at 2s. a stone, veal at 2d. a lb. and pork and mutton at $3\frac{1}{4}$d. Details are scarce, however, because Lady Fitzwalter paid the weekly household bill and recovered the money from Fitzwalter who entered the totals only; these, over the years, 1725–41, averaged £19. Two loose household bills have been preserved in the account books; one of these is for July 14th–22nd, 1738—

	£	s.	d.
Butcher	3	13	9
Grocer	2	9	$6\frac{3}{4}$
Washerwoman	2	12	9
Miller		18	0
Baker		8	5
"Rolls"		7	0
Mrs. Dwinger (*Housekeeper*) ...	1	8	6
Cook	1	7	6
	13	5	$5\frac{3}{4}$

It is well below average because it was for a period when the family was at Moulsham Hall, not at the Town house.

There are also several entries in the one account book which deals solely with expenditure at Moulsham Hall. For instance, for several years running, Edward Johnson, the steward, attended Braintree Fair in September. In 1734 he bought 10 cwts. of Gloucestershire cheese at five farthings a lb., and 50 lbs. of salt butter at $4\frac{3}{4}$d. Occasionally, Colchester oysters were bought at 3s. 6d. to 3s. 10d. a barrel and a collar of brawn, 30–49 lbs. in weight, at a penny a lb.

Drink

Fitzwalter's method of keeping accounts (see *Introduction*) left him with many blank left hand pages in his account books. These he used for matters and events which he considered important. Drink, especially wine, was one of these: there are a number of entries like the following—

"Memorand. Jan(*ua*)ry 14th, 1737. I bottled off one H.Hd. of Clarret from Combstock of Boulogne—it runn 21½ Dozen bottles."

The bottling, in fact, would be carried out by his butler, but it is highly likely that Fitzwalter would be watching. He certainly scrutinised the custom duties and other charges at the ports—he possessed "a custom-house book of Wine-Tables calculated". He probably watched the annual brewing of beer at Moulsham, and he was not above making a spot check on the Moulsham beer cellar.

He certainly liked his wine; it was almost the only commodity on which he spent freely and willingly, but, characteristically, if it were not to his taste it went back promptly to the shippers at Calais or Boulogne. He lived long before vintage years were invented, but he knew enough to go to the best shippers and importers, and he bought wines from the best districts, even though he attached little importance to mere names!—

"Bottled off a H.Hd. of Clarret here w(*hi*)ch runn Twenty one Dozen and a half large Bottles. The wine cost me 11 Guineas p(*er*) H.Hd. at Calais and was sent me by Monsr. Pigault from the Cellar of Monsr. Le Neau there. He calls it Chatteaux Margo."

During the years, 1725-41, he spent an average of £200 a year on wines. Claret was easily his favourite drink, accounting for about £90 a year on average. Its prime cost varied from about £15 a hogshead (sometimes £3 or £4 less) to about £23. Custom duty, together with port dues and incidental payments, ran to just over two-thirds of the prime cost; thus the final cost per hogshead usually ranged from £26 to £36. In the late 1740s, some consignments cost as much as £45, including duty; this was probably a result of the war with France. The capacity of a hogshead varied; it was larger than a modern hogshead, usually around 60 gallons, the size of a modern hogshead of cider. It usually ran to about 22 dozen bottles. Occasionally he bought bottled claret from wine merchants, this (as he probably knew well!) was expensive, varying from £2 2s. to £2 9s. a dozen. Names are not frequently mentioned: Chateau Margaux occurs several times and Latour once. Like most 18th century gentlemen, he referred to the red Graves from the area south of Bordeaux as "Pontac" or "Pontac claret".

Port came next, an average annual expenditure of £40–£45. Red port cost £20 a hogshead, sometimes a little less; white port was £14–£15. It is interesting to note that he uses "White Port" and "White Lisbon" as synonymous terms—there was a good deal of fortified wine being produced at that time in the vineyards inland from Lisbon.

Rhenish wine, as he called it, was a poor third, accounting for about £15 a year on average, and mainly already bottled; this he usually obtained from Ludovic Schart, the King's cellarman. Occasionally Moselle is mentioned, but it is not unlikely that Fitz-walter sometimes included this in the term "Rhenish". Next came Burgundy, Madeira and the Rhone wines from famous districts—Côte Rôtie and Hermitage. Burgundy cost £35–£39 a hogshead with duty; the Rhone wines, those southern burgundies, were about the same price as his claret; Madeira was cheap, about £1 a dozen.

He bought sack at about 15s. a dozen; brandy cost him 7s. 6d. to 9s. 6d. a gallon; during the 17 years of accounts analysed he bought a few gallons of arrack, an occasional hogshead of cider, a little mountain wine and just one bottle of Irish whisky. Two other rather interesting single purchases were 7 dozen and nine pints of red Cape wine and 5 dozen of Tavel. His bottles cost him £1 10s. to £1 12s. 6d. a gross, but he would not pay the extra 6s. a gross to have his coronet stamped on them. Incidentally, a gross of bottles, a fragile commodity, was 13 dozen!

In Fitzwalter's household beer was important. It was the staple drink of most of his personal servants and doubtless for all who worked in a lowly capacity on the small home farm at Moulsham Hall, but not those who sat at his steward's table! On May 14th, 1733, he paid £49 12s. to Richard Dighton of Great Baddow for malt for the year, March 1732–March 1733. This was used for ten brewings producing 30 hogsheads of ale and 70 of small beer, a noble sight in the Moulsham cellar.

He spent an average of £43 a year on tea, coffee and chocolate. From 1725 to 1740 he patronised the shop at the Sign of the White Greyhound in Fleet Street. At first this was run by a Mr. Humphrey Thayer, then by Thayer and Knollys; then by Richard Knollys alone; then by Knollys and Robinson, and finally by William Robinson alone. Sometimes they rendered quarterly bills, but usually an annual account. No details are given: a bill would simply state, for example, "Pd. Mr. Knollys, Druggist, his bill in full for Coffee, Tea, Chocolate &ca to Mich(*ael*)mas last past; 39–19–0". Thus it is not possible to know Fitzwalter's particular taste in coffee; indeed, the word disappears from all entries after 1735. With tea and chocolate it is different. In August 1740, before he finally dropped Robinson, he began to patronize Colet Maw-hood at the Golden Lion in the Strand. It is most likely that he called personally about every fortnight, collected the goods and, of course, a detailed receipted bill! One of these bills is preserved, loose, in Fitzwalter's last account book; it probably records the last time, June 11th, 1752, that he entered Mawhood's shop—the later entries, only three in number, state that Mawhood was paid by the house porter. There was little variation in price over the years, 1740–52. Chocolate remained steady at 5s. to 5s. 6d. a pound; Hyson tea was around 20s. a pound, ordinary green tea was 16s. and Bohea 14s. or up to 18s. for special quality.

Food and Drink—selective extracts
Original spelling retained

		£	s.	d.
1724	Dec. 15th			
	By return to John Ovens at Bristol for 2 H(*ogs*)h(*ea*)ds of French Claret	46	3	0
1725	Mar. 4th			
	To Johnson my butler a Bill of Expences abt. 2 H(*ogs*)h(*ea*)ds of wine from Bristol	5	16	2
	Aug. 17th			
	To 2 Gross of Long Neck'd Bottles to Bottle off a H(*ogs*)h(*ea*)d of Clarret ...	3	12	0
1726	Jan. 16th			
	To the Boys at St. James's Coffee House ...	1	1	0
1727	Feb. 1st			
	To Mr. Graves for 21 Dozen and half of Flasks of Pontack-Clarrett	48	0	0
	11th			
	To Mr. Knollys of the White Grey Hound in Fleetstreet in full for Coffee, Tea &ca for one Q(*uarte*)r ending Xstmas last ...	9	10	0

		£	s.	d.

June 10th

To a bill of exchange from Monsr. Mollieu at Calais for 15 Doz. of Clarret, 3 Doz. of Hermitage & 2 Doz. of Côte Rotee, £19–19–0, and for the Custom duty and expences at the Port of London on landing it, £14 8s. 34 7 0

14th

To Mr. Knollys, Druggist, for Coffee, Tea, Chocolate and Spaw-waters for one Q(uarte)r end(in)g 24th June last past ...   16 15 6

1728 Apr. 30th

To Mr. Schartz the King's Cellar-man for 4 Doz. of Rhenish wine at 3s. 6d. per bottle, and in full of all acco(un)ts ...   4 10 0

May 23rd

Pd. to Monsr. Smitzman for 8 Doz. of Rhenish-wine at 2s. 6d. p(er) Bottle ...   12 0 0

Nov. 21st

Pd. a bill of Exchange drawn upon me by Mr. Mollieu to George Fitzgerald and pd. to his servant, James Sandford, for 2 H(ogs)h(ea)ds of Clarret and one half H(ogs)h(ea)d of Hermitage & one half H(ogs)h(ea)d of Côte Rôtee, prime cost with the bottles, in all 79 7 0

1729 Nov. 11th

Pd. Mr. Mitford by the hands of Sam(ue)ll Johnson, Porter, Monsr. Mollieu's bill of Exchange for 2 H(ogs)h(ea)ds of Clarret, Bo(ugh)t in Dec(embe)r 1st last past at 18 Guineas per H(ogs)h(ea)d 37 16 0

1730 Apr. 21st

Pd. Mr. Cutler for 5 G(allon)s of Bat(avia) Arrack and 5 G(allon)s of Brandy sent into the Country 5 2 6

1731 Jan. 2nd

Short, the King's Cellar-man, for 16 Dozen of Rhenish-wine & Package for part of it into the Country, paying also for the Bottles and in full 26 6 0

		£	s.	d.
Mar. 16th To Dean Lockyer for 3 Doz. Qts. of Mountain Wine		1	14	9
1732 Jan. 7th To Mr. Warwick for the King's Duty for one H(*ogs*)h(*ea*)d of Clarret and all other Importation Expences for Two others, one of wch. was for the Count, £15 16s. 6d., and gave him for his trouble, £1 1s.		16	17	6
Aug. 12th Pd. Mr. Cavalery, Confectioner, his bill in full		11	9	9
Nov. 13th Came to Town—Spent at Romford, £1, and bo(*ugh*)t a Cheshire cheese there, w(*eigh*)t 50 lb. at 4½d. *p*(*er*) pound, came to eighteen shillings and 5d.		1	18	5
Dec. 13th Pd. Mr. Warwick his Bill of Expences for the Import duty &ca on Three H(*ogs*)h(*ea*)ds of La Tour wine imported from Calais, £39 11s. 7d. and for his own trouble, £1 1s.		40	12	7
1733 May 14th Pd. — Dighton of Baddow, Malster, his bill for Malt beginning the 28th of March, 1732, and ending March 28th, 1733, being for Ten Brewings, viz. each Brewing, 3 H(*ogs*)h(*ea*)ds of Ale and 7 H(*ogs*)h(*ea*)ds of small beer, w(*hi*)ch is Ten in all, and am(*oun*)ts in the whole year to 100 H(*ogs*)h(*ea*)ds, pd. him in full to the 28th of March last inclusive		49	12	0
1734 Jan. 4th Pd. Mr. Kelsal at the Red Lion at Chelmsford in full for seven Barr(*e*)lls of Oysters from Colchester		1	7	1

	£	s.	d.

June 20th

Pd. Mr. Alexand(e)r Lyon, £25, by bill of Exchange for Monsr. Mollieu at Calais for a H(*ogs*)h(*ea*)d of Pontack-Clarret, rec(*eive*)d by me this last June 8th from sd. Mollieu, viz. pd. in mony, £11 15s. 4½d. and by bill and rec(*eip*)t of £13 4s. 7½d., pd. by me for Custom duty &ca on a H(*ogs*)h(*ea*)d of Clarret imported the 27th of April last past and now return'd by me not lik(*ing*) the sd. wine, in all, £25   **11   15   4½**

Sept. 25th

Pd. — Jeoffries the Malster of Bexfields for three Brewings of Malt, viz., one of 35 Bushels and Two of 38 Bushels each at 3s. p(er) Bushel, & in full of all acco(*un*)ts   **16   16   0**

26th

Pd. Johnson my steward for 1000 wt. of Gloucester-shire bo(*ugh*)t at Braintree fair at abt. five farthings *p(er)* pound and 50 lb wt. of salt-butter at abt. 4d. 3 farthings **7   15   6**

Oct. 1st

Pd. Hewes for bringing 1100 w(*ei*)ght of Cheese from Braintree-fair **7   0**

Nov. 19th

Bottl'd off a H(*ogs*)h(*ea*)d of Clarret here w(*hi*)ch runn Twenty one Dozen and a half large Bottles. The wine cost me 11 Guineas *p(er)* H(*ogs*)h(*ea*)d at Calais and was sent me by Monsr. Pigault from the Cellar of Monsr. Le Neau there. He calls calls it Chatteaux Margo.

Dec. 9th

Pd. Rich(*ar*)d Plater for Two Hoggs that were kill'd in the house this month, one for Bacon, the other for Pickel'd Pork at (*blank*) *p(er)* stone **4   12   9**

| | £ | s. | d. |

1735 Jan. 11th

Pd. Mr. Vanderstegen, by the hands of John Parsons his Book-keeper, for one H(*ogs*)h(*ea*)d of white-Port sent in Feb-(*rua*)ry 16th, 1733, £15, April 12th. To one H(*ogs*)h(*ea*)d of Red-port sent to Moulsham-Hall, £20. To one H(*ogs*)-h(*ea*)d of White-Port at the same time to Moulsham, £15. To one H(*ogs*)h(*ea*)d of White Port, Sept. 20th, sent also to Moulsham, £15, and in full of all acco(*un*)ts to this day **65 0 0**

Feb. 12th

Pd. James Edm(*un*)ds for Mathews and Co. for 30 Mellon Glasses & Packing sent down to Moulsham Hall, £2. 9s. 2d. and for eight Gross of Moulded quart-Bottles, Thirteen to the Doz., £12. N.B. if stamp'd w(*i*)th a Coronet, 6s. *p*(*er*) Gross more ... **14 9 2**

Mar 18th

Pd. John Cooling at the Bunch of Grapes Tavern in King's-Street St. James's Square in part of a bill deliver'd in for wine for my steward's Table of £41. 8s. 3d. Pd. on acco(*un*)t £21 ... ... **21 0 0**

May 17th

Pd. Mr. Honour the Custom-duty and Charges on the importation of a H(*ogs*)-h(*ea*)d of Clarret w(*hi*)ch was Gaug'd at 61 Gallons from George Gordon at Bou-logne. Pd. by the hands of — Turner, my Butler **13 10 10**

Aug. 22nd

Bottl'd off a Hogshead of white Lisbon, had of Mr. Vandersteegen, w(*hi*)ch runn 19 Doz. But there was 3 Doz. and ½ drunk from the H(*ogs*)h(*ea*)d, so that it con-tain'd in the whole, 22 Doz. ¼.

Oct. 10th   £   s.   d.

Bottl'd off a H(*ogs*)h(*ea*)d of strong-Beer, having drunk of it some days before, so that it runn but 19 Dozen. It was Brew'd in Oct. last, being 1734, and is now one year old.

Nov. 20th

Pd. to Capt. Gilbe for a H(*ogs*)h(*ea*)d of Clarret, Monsr. Pigault, £15 –s. 6d. and for duty on Landing, £13 6s. 6d., and for freight and Primage, 11s. in all   28   18   0

1736   May 29th

Pd. Mr. Vanderstegen, Portugal Wine-Merch(*an*)t, by the hands of his serv(*an*)t John Parsons, his bill for wine in full, viz., for 4 H(*ogs*)h(*ea*)ds of White Lisbon, £60, for one H(*ogs*)h(*ea*)d of Red Port, £20, for 3 Doz. Bottles of Red Port, £2 10s. in all   82   10   0

1737   Jan. 12th

Pd. Import duty and other expenses on landing half a H(*ogs*)h(*ea*)d of Burgundy (vin de Nuys) from Monsr. Mollieu at Calais, and bringing it home   ...   7   2   0

Feb. 5th

To a bill of Exchange drawn upon me by Lewis and Gasper Mollieu to G. Fitz-Gerald & comp(*an*)y for half a H(*ogs*)-h(*ea*)d of Burgundy, from Calais   ...   10   10   0

Nov. 1st

Pd. by the hands of the Earl of Ancram to Messrs. Alexander and Coates as by letter from Mr. Shairp at Edinburgh for three H(*ogs*)h(*ea*)ds of French Clarret sent by him to me last sum(*m*)er, and in full of all acco(*un*)ts   111   10   10

1738   Apr. 10th

John Spillman for a Collar of Brawn sent to London at Christmas last, wt. 49lb. Pd. in full   2   9   0

	£	s.	d.

Apr. 24th
Pd. Sam(*ue*)ll Towers of the King's Cellar
his bill in full for 12 Doz. and a half of
Rhenish-wine at £1 12s. 6d. *p*(*er*) Doz.
and for Porters and Hampers for the
country 20 14 0

May 25th
Pd. Ph. Gostal for 9 Doz. of Herefordshire
Syder and 4 Bottles at 6s. *p*(*er*) Doz. and
3 Hampers, in full 2 19 0

27th
Pd. for 6 Doz. Pints of sack sent down into
Essex by Thos. Flowers, and in full ...   4 8 10

June 27th
When I came down hither, June 27th, 1735,
I found in my Cellar 27 H(*ogs*)h(*ea*)ds of
small beer.

1739 Jan. 16th
Pd. Knollys and Robinson in Fleet-Street,
Druggists, their bill in full for Tea,
Chocolate, Pyrmont-Water &ca from
Oct. 6th, 1737, to Sept(*embe*)r 1st, 1738   42 2 10

Feb. 1st
Pd. Mr. Tindal for a H(*ogs*)h(*ea*)d of the
sower-water cyder he sent for me out (*of*)
Devonshire, with the Carriage to London   2 16 0

Mar. 15th
Pd. Mich(*ael*) Edw(*ard*) of Rotterdam for
7 Dozen and nine pints of Red Cape
Wine by bill on me payable to John
Goddard, and in full 21 2 8

1740 Feb. 18th
To John Parsons, Clerk to Mr. Vanderstegen, his bill in full to Nov. 3rd, 1738,
for 2 H(*ogs*)h(*ea*)ds of white port, £30,
for one, H(*ogs*)h(*ea*)d of red port, £18,
and for the H(*ogs*)h(*ea*)d of sherry, £15
in all 63 0 0

		£	s.	d.

June 6th
> Pd. John Page, Wine-Merch(*an*)t for 4 Doz. of Clarret, for 1 Doz. of Champaigne, and for five Doz. of a French wine he calls Tavelle &ca, and in full of all acco(*un*)ts — **22 2 0**

Aug. 20th
> Pd. Mr. Mawhood, at the Golden-Lyon in the Strand, for one pd. of Hyson-Tea, £1, for one pd. of fine Green, 16s., and for one pd. of the finest flower of Bohea, 18s., Cannisters 1s. 6d., in full ... ... — **2 15 6**

30th
> Pd. Johnson for 2 Boxes of Eringo root, and Carriage ... ... — **10 0**

1741 Feb. 25th
> Pd. Mr. Charles Smith of Boulogne for 3 H(*ogs*)h(*ea*)ds of wine and in full of all acco(*un*)ts, £56 18s., he having also allow'd £14(?) 2s. for freight, Port and Import duties on a H(*ogs*)h(*ea*)d of Burgundy w(*hi*)ch I returned upon his hands, one H(*ogs*)h(*ea*)d of Burgundy, £20, one of Clarret, £23, one of Pontac, £28. Pd. in full ... ... — **56 18 0**

Apr. 21st
> Pd. Mrs. Allen her bill in full for 3 Doz. of Hermitage at £2 5s. *p*(*er*) Doz. and for 2 Doz of Cotte rotie at do., & for other wines, in full of all acco(*un*)ts ... ... — **12 9 0**

May 24th
> Pd. the Earl of Holdernesse for a H(*ogs*)h(*ea*)d of Dorchester beer, £4 1s., and for half a H(*ogs*)h(*ea*)d of Red Champagne w(*hi*)ch is still in my Lord's Cellar, £12 8s. 5d. ... ... — **16 9 5**

1744 Jan. 27th
> Pd. Mat. Blackiston, Grocer, for 2 Gallons of Batavia-Arrack ... ... — **1 1 0**

	£	s.	d.

Nov.

 Pd. at the Custom-house, Nov(*embe*)r 1744, the Duty on 380 Gallons of Moselle-wine for the Earl of Holdernesse at 2s. 6d. *p*(*er*) Gallon, £46 16s. 7d.

Nov.

 Pd. also to Mr. Mears for carrying it down to Moulsham-Hall, £2 5s.

 Pd. also to Mr. Schaartz for four Doz. of Moselle to fill up the Barrells (*not entered*).

May 13th

 Pd. an old bill of my Lady Fitzwalter's at Mrs. Margasse's for India sweet meats, £3 –s. 3d., and laid out £3 more 6 0 3

1748 Jan. 16th

 Pd. Mr. Law(*rence*) Dundas on account of a bill delivered in of £349 14s. 6d. Pd. him this day 300 0 0
N.B. But as the greater part of this wine stands charg'd at £45 *p*(*er*) H(*ogs*)h(*ea*)d, he has agreed to reduce it all to £42 *p*(*er*) H(*ogs*)h(*ea*)d.

1749 May 1st

 Pd. John Hunt of Bath by the hands of Walter Dicker for six Dozen of Mountain wine, and in full 8 0 0

1753 Nov. 28th

 Pd. at the Custom-house Fees there w(*i*)th the duty due on a Pipe of Madera-wine, from Governor Thomas 14 8 0
Pd. also last month, £22, for sd. Pipe of Madera, a bill drawn upon me by the sd. Gov(*erno*)r Thomas 22 0 0

(c) *Furniture and Furnishings*

It may seem that Fitzwalter spent only modestly on furniture and furnishings. This is not strictly true. When he and Lady Holderness were married in 1724 they were not a young couple faced with heavy expenditure in setting up house from scratch. He walked into a splendid town house, his wife's, in Pall Mall, and it is reasonable to assume that her father, Meinhardt, Duke of Schomberg, had furnished it in keeping with the high standard he had displayed in remodelling the fabric. It was only when the Fitzwalters were preparing to move from Popes, their modest country house, to the growing splendour of their new Moulsham Hall that there was need for a fair amount of new furnishing. The recorded annual average spent on furniture and furnishings is £82, and even allowing for omissions and the loss of one Moulsham account book, the true average must have been under £100. The heaviest years are 1730–32 (average, £246) when the new East and South wings were ready for occupation. For the years, 1746–48, when Moulsham was nearing completion, the average was again high (£158).

The craftsman most heavily and continuously employed was Samuel Bolar (or Boler), a London cabinet maker, quite unknown to authorities on 18th century furniture. He had been employed by Lady Fitzwalter before her marriage to Fitzwalter. The last payment was made to him on May 27th, 1737, but payments to a Samuel Boler, corn chandler, began in October 1739, and continued throughout the rest of the account books. The total paid to him in the years, 1724–37, was £934 15s. 0d.; this represents 58% of *all* payments on furniture and fittings during those years, and should also be set against the £2,466 which is the grand, recorded total for the whole period of the account books, 1724–54. Maybe, Fitzwalter patronised him because he was relatively inexpensive. This may never be established: no details of his commissions have survived. It is quite certain, however, that he was *good*; otherwise Fitzwalter would not have employed him.

All other cabinet makers patronised by Fitzwalter were apparently not commissioned; he probably called at their shops and bought off the peg. They were

George Nix (King Street, Covent
    Garden) ...   .   6 payments, total £44 3s.

Daniel Bell and Thomas Moore (St. Martin's lane)	3 payments, total £49 1s.
Jarman (York Street, Covent Garden)	1 payment, total £6 18s.
Elkunah Haddock (Greek Street)	1 payment, total £15
Luke Stevenson	2 payments, total £2 8s.
Richard Pickhaver, or Pickhaven (St. Martin's Court)	5 payments, total £14 13s. 6d., for card tables
William Dunton	2 payments, total £19

There were also payments to George Murray, carver, once described as carver and cabinet maker.

In the early years of the account books, before he succeeded his brother, Fitzwalter patronised Thomas Arne, upholsterer, of the Crown, King Street. He was the father of the famous composer. In later years he made heavy payments to various upholsterers—

Lancaster Noone (Chelmsford)	£77 9s. 5d.
How (Chelmsford; probably Noone's successor)	£120 15s. 11d.
William Bradshaw	£419 2s. 8½d.
Sam. Jones (Pall-Mall)	£251 2s. 1d.
William Spurret (St. James's Street)	£74 8s. 0d.

Carpets bought by Fitzwalter are variously described as "Tapestry-worked", Brussels, Tournai, Turkish, French, £78 10s. 6d. in all. On March 5th, 1734, he paid £5 14s. 6d. "for a Turkey carpet the day Sir Robert Walpole and the Duke of Newcastle, etc., dined with me".

Furniture and furnishings—Transcript of all relevant entries
Original spelling retained

		£	s.	d.
1724	Nov. 26th			
	For a little Persian carpet	2	10	0
1725	Jan. 13th			
	To Mr. Bolar on an old bill of my Lady Holdernesse's due before the 18th of June last	14	7	0
	20th			
	To Mr. Arne, upholster, being an old bill of my wife's. Pd. in full	15	15	0

		£	s.	d.
Feb. 22nd				
To an old Bill of my wife's for mats &ca ...		7	0	0
Aug. 18th				
To Mr. Bolar on acco(un)t and in part of a bill due		50	0	0
Sept. 11th				
To Mrs. Tailors for a little screen & Tea-board		1	12	0
1726 Nov. 17th				
For a little Persian Carpet		1	16	0
30th				
For five pieces of Ind(ian) Damask to Lady Holdernesse for the Drawing-room, having bought three before		45	0	0
1727 Apr. 10th				
To Mr. Sam(ue)ll Bolar's bill of £302 17s. deliver'd in of w(hi)ch £50 pd. April 1725, and in farther part paid this day £100 ...		100	0	0
Dec. 2nd				
To Sam(ue)ll Bolar the further sum of fifty in part of a bill already given in of £302 17s., of which £150 was paid before, remains now due, £100 17s.		50	0	0
20th				
To Mr. Arne, upholder, in full of a bill for for the funeral of my son Schonberg, of £36 15s. 6d., & of all acco(un)ts		16	15	6
1728 Feb. 2nd				
To Nix the Joyner in Covent Gardens for a 3 square table to write upon		2	2	0
Mar. 29th				
To Mr. Bolar in full of his bill given in of £302 17s.		52	0	0
Oct. 2nd				
For a 2-Leaved Paper screen bot. in Pauls Church yard			15	0
Dec. 19th				
To — Fletcher in Pauls Church yard for a Gilt Leather, skreen sent down to Moulsham Hall		1	7	0

		£	s.	d.
1729	Feb. 10th			
	To a Carpet Bought at an auction ...	2	15	0
	June 13th			
	To Mr. Bolar in part of his bill of	20	0	0
	Dec. 13th			
	Pd. Mr. Nix for an Easie-chair	5	0	0
	22nd			
	Bt. off and pd. Mr. Ellis, partner w(ith) Mr. Vanderbank in great Queen's street for a tapestry work'd carpet	10	10	0
1730	Jan. 2nd			
	Pd. Mr. Cutler for 6 peices of Chinse to make beds for Moulsham Hall	(not entered)		
	To Ditto for Four French Carpets tack'd together	5	0	0
	Jan. 16th			
	Pd. Mr. Sam(ue)ll Bolar in part of his bill of £39 11s.	25	4	0
	17th			
	To Mr. Cutler for Nine peices of Chinse for a bed & for a (?) Ham, ½ a guinea ...	25	14	6
	Mar. 10th			
	To Mr. Roberts of Bartolmew-Close for 6 Dutch Chairs & packing sent to Moulsham	2	0	0
	Apr. 16th			
	To Wildey at the Toy-shop by Pauls for an Indian skreen for Moulsham	2	16	0
	21st			
	Pd. Mr. Cutler for a Quilting	3	15	0
	To/do/for peices of Belting	2	12	0
	To/do/for a little Brussels Carpet	1	5	0
	May 1st			
	Pd. Mr. Cutler for a peice of French Carpetting, 14 yds in length	3	5	0

	£	s.	d.

May 16th
Pd. Mr. Nix Cabinet-maker for a Close-stool w(*ith*) a Leather Top and for a Corner Cupboard upon 3 legs to send down to Moulsham Hall, £1 15s. each, in all ... ... — 3 10 0

20th
To Mr. Cutler for a Chinese Counterpane and in full of all acco(*un*)ts ... ... — 4 4 0

July 17th
Pd. Rob(*ert*) Broumhead in Pauls Church-yard at the Red Lyon for a windsor Chair with 4 seats ... ... — 1 4 0

Aug. 12th
To Mr. Sam(*ue*)ll Boler Cabinet-maker, on acco(*un*)t for work done to(*wards*) furnishing at Moulsham Hall ... ... — 50 0 0

Oct. 20th
Pd. for a Chess-Board, £1 5s., for the men, 19s. ... ... — 2 0 0
(*sic*)

Dec. 18th
Pd. Mr. Sam(*ue*)ll Boler on acco(*un*)t, £25, having before pd. him £50 ... ... — 25 0 0

24th
To Mr. Nix, Cabinet-maker, in full his bill — 10 0 0

1731 Jan. 26th
To Mr. Cutler for a Tournay Carpet sufficient to go round Two beds, Moulsham — 3 5 0

Feb. 26th
To Mr. Valensia a Jew, for Two Marble Tables, one of purple the other of Black and Yellow marble, con(*taining*) abt. 18 foot at 6s. *p(er)* ft. ... ... — 5 11 0

Apr. 27th
Pd. Mr. Noon in part of a bill of £24 for upholster's work ... ... — 10 10 0

	£	s	d.

May 6th
Pd. to a man in Pauls Ch.-yard for a Leather fire-skreen on a stand ... ... — 1 6 0

24th
Pd. Mr. Vicars on acco(*un*)t for a Large quantity of yellow-mohair sent down to Moulsham to furnish the best apartment — 100 0 0

26th
To Mrs. Toomes and — an Indian Chest to be sent down to Moulsham ... ... — 16 5 6

27th
To Mr. Bolar, Cabinet maker and upholster, on acco(*un*)t ... ... — 50 0 0

July 4th
Pd. Mr. Noon of Chelmsford, upholster, in full of his bill of £24 4s. 4d., having pd. him £10 10s. before, to June 30, 1730 ... — 13 14 4

13th
Pd. Mr. Goude, stone-Mason for a purple marble slab for a Table of 5 foot 10 inches long and 2 foot 7 inches wide, at 7s. 6d. *p(er)* foot ... ... — 5 13 2

Sept. 1st
To Mr. Noone, upholster, in full of his bill to this day ... ... — 18 16 9

Dec. 24th
Pd. Mr. Sam(*ue*)ll Bolar, Cabinet-maker, in part of a bill just bro(*ugh*)t in of (*blank*) for goods sent down to Moulsham Hall and for work done there ... ... — 100 0 0

1732 Feb. 9th
To W(*illia*)m Rodwell near Ludgate in full for Two Window blinds of Canvas, Mosaic Gilt ... ... — 4 3 0

23rd
Pd. James Tooly for four Window blinds for Moulsham Hall, bill deliver'd, £7 7s. 6d. pd. in part ... ... — 5 5 0

	£	s.	d.
Mar. 7th			
Pd. James Tooley in full for his window blinds	2	2	0
Mar 24th			
Pd. Jos(e)p(h) Jervis for a piece of Diaper, for 2 Pier Glasses, for Cheney-Pots (for) flowers, bot. at an auction at Dover House, Cox Auctioneer	34	17	1
Apr. 19th			
Pd. Mr. Gousset, Carver, in full for a Large frame of a Table and for Two frames for my wife's and my Pictures at full length at Moulsham	19	4	6
June 5th			
Pd. Mr. Nix, Cabinet-maker, in full ...	15	11	0
22nd			
To my Lady Fitzwalter for a Dozen soope China Plates	1	10	0
Oct. 3rd			
Pd. Lancaster Noone in full of his bill and of all acco(un)ts	5	19	0
Nov. 18th			
Pd. Mr Sam(ue)ll Bolar, Cabinet-maker, further on acco(un)t of a bill deliver'd for work done and goods sent down to Moulsham Hall	100	0	0
Dec. 13th			
Pd. Bell and Moore their bill in full for a large Glass, and dining chairs with Blew Leather, Ten in no. sent down to Moulsham Hall	33	6	0
20th			
To Mr. W(illia)m Waters, Frame maker and Gilder, pd. his bill in full for Two Carv'd and Gilded frames for marble slabs for the Drawing-room and Bed-chamber at Moulsham Hall, £14, for an Oval Frame and Gilding & Carving it, and a Glass for the N. East room below-stairs, £4 10s.			

		£	s	d.
1733 May 2nd Pd. Bell & Moore Cabinet makers, on acco(*un*)t, the sum of Ten Pounds in part of a bill of £11 or thereab(*ou*)ts, the bill being mislaid		10	0	0
June 16th To Mr. Waters for a Large looking-Glass and large Gilt Frame for the North-East dining-room at Moulsham, w(*i*)th the package &ca and in full of all acco(*un*)ts		34	1	0
19th Pd. Mr. Sam(*ue*)ll Bolar in farther part of his bill the sum of		50	0	0
Aug. 22nd Pd. Lanc. Noone, the upholsterer, his bill in full		16	9	8
Sept. 7th Pd. Mr. Boler in farther part of his bill deliver'd in		25	0	0
1734 Feb. 26th To — Moore and Bell, To a Walnut-Tree Desk w(*i*)th 4 Drawers		5	15	0
28th Pd. Mr. Sam(*ue*)ll Boler, Cabinet maker, in farther part of his bill given in for goods sent down last year to Moulsham Hall ...		25	0	0
Mar. 5th For a Turky carpit the day S(*i*)r Rob(*er*)t Walpole and the Duke of Newcastle &ca din'd w(*i*)th me		5	14	6
Apr. 20th Pd. Mr. Boler, Cabinet-Maker, in farther part of his bill for work done and goods sent down to Moulsham Hall. N.B. According to a note he gave me in today, there still remains due on sd. bill, £28 1s. 1½d.		25	0	0

		£	s.	d.

Aug. 1st
Pd. Mr. Boler, Cabinet maker, in farther part of his bill deliver'd in, £20, so that there remains due to him now only the sum of £8 1s. 1½d. ... ... — 20 0 0

Sept. 4th
Pd. Lancaster Noone, upholster at Chelmsford, his bill in full of all acco(*un*)ts ... — 12 4 0

Nov. 20th
Pd. Gainge, Joyner, for a mohogony dining table of 4 ft. 3 ins. by 5 feet ... ... — 2 12 6

1735 July 25th
Pd. Mr. Sam(*ue*)ll Boler, Cabinet-maker, in part of a bill deliver'd in May 9, 1735, of 128, pd. this day ... ... — 50 0 0

Nov. 5th
Pd. to — Cox in Covent Garden for a Large Turkey Carpet ... ... — 5 16 0

1736 Jan. 28th
Pd. Mr. Sam(*ue*)ll Boler, Cabinet maker, in farther part of his bill, £50, so that there now remains £20 due ... ... — 50 0 0

Apr. 13th
Pd. Jarman in York-street Covent Garden for a Mohogony Chest of 4 drawers for Cloaths, w(*i*)th castors, £4 16s., and for a mohogony long square table for Ten people, £2 2s. ... ... — 6 18 0

1737 Feb. 11th
Pd. Mr. — Jones, upholster in the Pall Mall on account of work done for me in this house in Pall Mall, viz. hanging the yellow drawing-room below-stairs. Putting up the Blew Mohair bed, and hanging the bed-chamber, one p(*air*) of stairs, and putting (*up*) the blew-mohair bed and hanging my Lord Holdernesses Bed Chamber, 2 p(*air*) of stairs. Pd. him in part of a bill given in of £64 17s. 6d. Pd. ... ... — 26 5 0

Apr. 30th   £   *s.*   *d.*

Pd. Elkunah Haddock of Greek-street, cabinet maker, for a Library-Table cover'd w(*i*)th green Cloth and w(*i*)th nine Drawers, and in full of all accounts   15   0   0

May 11th

Pd. Mr. Jones, upholsterer in the Pall Mall, in farther part of his bill given in of £64 17s. 6d., of w(*hi*)ch I have before pd £26 5s., and now £22, so that there remains £16 12s.   22   0   0

27th

To Mr. Boler, Cabinet-maker, in full of his bill of £128, £28, having pd. him £100 before at Two several paym(*e*)nts, and in full of all demands   28   0   0

(This is the last payment to S.B., cabinet-maker. The first payment to S.B., corn chandler, was made on October 20th, 1739.)

June 16th

Pd. Luke Stephenson, Cabinet-maker, his bill in full   1   10   6

July 19th

Pd. Mr. How of Chelmsford, upholster, his bill in full for pulling down and setting up beds and furniture when the boards were new laid, &ca   15   19   8

29th

Pd. Sam. Jones, upholster, the sum of £16 12s. 6d. in full satisfaction of his bill of £64 7s. 6d., pd. the rest before   16   12   6

Dec. 29th

Pd. Sam. Jones, upholster, £13 13s. on acco(*un*)t of a bill deliver'd in of £43 10s. 6d., goods sent to Hampton Court ...   13   13   0

1738 Feb. 28th

Bot. at Mrs. Dawson's Two Japan Boards for tea, chocolate &ca   1   4   0

	£	s.	d.

Apr. 11th
Pd. Sam. Jones, upholsterer, in farther part of his bill of £43, £10 10s., having paid him before, £13 13s., so that there now remains due to him, £20, wanting three ten shillings (*sic*) 10 10 0

June 27th
Pd. —, the Pump maker at Moulsham for 2 Windsor Chairs for the Garden. Just deliver'd 2 0 0

Aug. 14th
Pd. Mr. Gainge, Joyner, for making a settee for my Dressing-room here, for wood and his work only 18 0

15th
Pd. Mr. How, upholsterer, for stuffing and a Case of Blew — for said settee ... (*not entered*)

1739 Jan. 24th
Pd. Luke Stephenson for a Dressing-Glass in the silver frame for the Countess Fitz-Walter 18 0

Mar. 5th
To Rich(*ar*)d Pick-haver, Cabinet-maker, for a large Card Table, £2 8s. &ca, his bill in full 3 4 6

June 30th
Pd. for a Bureau. Trim'd and inlay'd w(*i*)th brass and bought at an auction by my wife 8 8 0

Aug. 8th
Pd. — Holford for a Windsor Chair for 3 people 1 0 0

Dec. 20th
Pd. Rich(*ar*)d Pick-haver for a square card table of mohogony cover'd w(*i*)th green cloth 2 2 0

		£	s.	d.

1740 May 28th

    Pd. Sam. Jones, upholster, his bill in full of £89 17s. 3d. having pd. him before on acco(un)t £25 8s. Pd. him this day and in full of all accounts **64 9 0**

June 5th

    Pd. My Lady Ancram for a Japan'd Tea-board made here, w(hi)ch she had pd. for me to Mrs. Sambrooke **1 11 6**

27th

    To Rob(er)t Shipman for a square matt for my Lady Fitz-Walter's China (?"*Chinse*") room **2 0 0**

Aug. 22nd

    Bt. a Commode for my Lady Ancram, cost **16 0**

Sept. 24th

    Pd. Mr. How of Chelmsford, upholster, on acco(un)t lately deliver'd in of £104 16s. 3½d., having pd. in pt. before, £52. Pd. in farther pt. this day, £30 more, so there remains due, £22 3s. 6d. **30 0 0**

1741 Jan. 9th

    Pd. Mr. Pickhaver, Joyner, for a square Card Table, £2 2s., for covering and mending 3 others, £1 15s. **3 15 0**
                                                       (sic)

Oct. 28th

    Pd. Mr. Pickhaver for a mohogony Card Table, and in full of all acco(un)ts ... **2 4 0**

Nov. 16th

    Pd. Sam. Jones, upholster, his bill for Bedding Chairs, &ca, in Bothmer's Meuse, and in full **7 15 0**

1742 Dec. 22nd

    Pd. Mr. Spurret, upholster, on account ... **10 10 0**

Dec. 26th

    Pd. Anth. Lucera for a Chest of Florence sent to Moulsham (*Is this furniture or wine?*) **4 10 6**

		£	s.	d.

1743 Jan. 27th

Pd. W(*illia*)m Dunton for the Frames of Chairs and Settees, and in full of all accounts **15 15 0**

Feb. 16th

Pd. Mr. Spurret in farther part of his bill deliver'd in **21 0 0**

Mar. 4th

Pd. Sam. Jones, upholster, for 2 Wilton Carpets for my House in Pall Mall, and in full **25 10 0**

26th

Pd. W(*illia*)m Spurret, upholster, his bill of £61 18s. 10d. in full, having this day paid him by the hands of W(*illia*)m Wilkins, £30 8s., and the rest before **30 8 0**

31st

Pd. W(*illia*)m Dunton & Co. for another Wallnut-Tree settee for the Drawing-room above-stairs, London, and in full ... **3 5 0**

1744 Feb. 2nd

Pd. Sam. Jones, upholster, his bill in full to this day **9 11 1**

Dec. 22nd

Pd. Peter Wallace for a Turkey Carpet, 15 ft. 2 ins. long **13 2 6**

1745 Jan. 7th

Pd. P. Wallace for a Turkey Carpet in full **5 10 0**

Jan. 30th

Pd. — Spurret, upholster, his bill in full ... **3 1 0**

Feb. 21st

Pd. Mr. Pickhaver for putting on a new Cloth and mending a Card Table, 10s., and for making one entirely new, £2 8s. **2 18 0**

Mar. 6th

Pd. Mr. Halett of Newport-street for Ten black leather bottom'd chairs for my dining room in town, and in full ... **17 10 0**

	£	s.	d.
May 14th			
Pd. Sam. Jones, upholster, his bill in full. Not pd.			
1746 Mar. 12th			
Pd. Mr. Hallett, upholster, his bill in full ...	9	19	0
Apr. 29th			
Pd. for a Pier-Glass bought at an auction	4	5	0
June 25th			
Pd. Jn. Prestage for a Mohogony writing-table for Moulsham Hall	4	10	0
30th			
Pd. Mr. W(*illia*)m Bradshaw, upholster, on account of a bill of £275 4s. 11d., deliver'd in to me, £100. Rests due in sd. bill, £175 4s. 11d.	100	0	0
July 28th			
Pd. Sam. Jones, upholster, his bill in full of all demands	5	1	0
July 31st			
Pd. Edward Newman for 2 spring Curtains for Moulsham Hall and in full	3	0	0
1746 July 31st			
Pd. Mr. — Heath for a Terrestrial-Globe, 17 inches Diameter, w(*i*)th a Leather Case, and in full	4	12	0
Aug. 2nd			
Pd. W(*illia*)m — for a night-Table w(*i*)th a close-stool, and in full of all accounts ...	2	10	0
1747 Feb. 18th			
Pd.. Geo. Murray, Carver & Cabinet-maker, for work done at Moulsham Hall, the sum of £20 on account of a bill of £48 17s. 6d., rests due, £28 17s. 6d.			
Memorand(*u*)m. Pd. Mr. W(*illia*)m Bradshaw, upholster, by bill on Messrs. Snow and Denne from Bath in Jan(*ua*)ry or Dec(*embe*)r 1746, the farther sum of £100, so that there rests due only £75 4s. 11d. on his bill of £275 4s. 11d.			

		£	s.	d.

Apr. 1st
Pd. Mr. Hallett for a little fire-screen and in full **1 1 0**

May 19th
Pd. Mr. Bradshaw, upholster, in full of his bill of £275 4s. 11d. **75 4 11**

July 17th
Pd. G. Murray, Carver, in full of his bill of £95 14s. 6d. and of all acco(*un*)ts the sum of £28 11s. **28 17 0**

		£	s.	d.

1748 Apr. 28th
Pd. Mr. W(*illia*)m Bradshaw, upholster, his bill in full, and in full of all accounts to this day **114 12 0**

May 17th
Pd. Mr. W(*illia*)m Hallett for a light fire-screen, and in full **1 1 0**

20th
Pd. Edw(*ar*)d Newman in Paul's Church-yard for six Windsor-Chairs, viz Two Double, four single ones **2 8 0**

Dec. 17th
Pd. — Murray, Carver, his bill in full ... **5 17 6**

1749 Dec. 11th
Pd. Mr. Richards, Carver, in full of his bill of £106 19s. **56 19 0**

1750 Jan. 18th
Pd. H. Steinfeild, a German Cabinet-maker, in full for a Mahogony Campaign-Desk and case to send it down in to Moulsham Hall **5 0 0**

Dec. 17th
Pd. H. Steinfeild for covering a Card-Table **13 6**

1751 Dec. 23rd
Pd. Mr. Bradshaw, upholster, his bill in full of all demands **139 19 9½**

		£	s.	d.
1752	Jan. 18th			
	Pd. H. Steinfeild for covering a Card-Table w(i)th green Cloth and in full		13	0
1753	Jan. 22nd			
	Pd. Mr. Moline for a round Mohog(an)y Claw-Table	1	3	0
	May 15th			
	Pd. Mr. Bradshaw for an easie-chair and 6 matted ones	3	18	0
	Nov. 16th			
	Pd. Mr. Bradshaw for a Turkey-Carpet, and full for that	10	0	0

CHAPTER FOUR

CLOTHING AND ACCESSORIES

Clothing

For several reasons it is impossible to estimate accurately how much Fitzwalter spent on clothing. Some of the reasons apply to all kinds of expenditure; some are peculiar to clothing—

(1) Fitzwalter's are not *audited* accounts, but his own personal record, and it is evident that he *did* forget from time to time to enter payments. But how often? If he paid, say, £35 on a £78 bill, did he forget to enter payment of the balance, or was this balance always brought forward when the next bill was rendered?

(2) He was away for long periods at spas, especially Bath. Usually only totals for his expenditure there are entered and sometimes these are merely his own rough estimates. On at least two occasions, possibly on every visit, he kept details of his expenditure at Bath in a separate "Bath book", which, alas, has not survived. However, it is not reasonable to suppose that Fitzwalter could stay in Bath and *not* spend money on clothes. It is significant that in 1749 and again in 1751 when the Fitzwalters visited Bath *and* Tunbridge Wells, the clothing payments are down compared with 1747, 1748, 1750, 1752 and 1753.

(3) His accounts do not always differentiate between his expenditure on himself and that on his servants, his step-children and on the children of his stepdaughter, Lady Ancram.

(4) The accounts do not always distinguish between his personal and household expenditure—how much linen, for example, was made up into shirts and how much went for household use?

(5) The missing Moulsham account book has been mentioned several times. Its loss is serious in estimating some forms of expenditure, but it is highly unlikely to have contained many entries of payment on clothes.

The account books show that in 30 years, Fitzwalter recorded expenditure totalling £10,601 5s. 7d. on clothes and textiles; this gives an annual average of £352 16s. It includes his own clothes, Lord Holderness's while he was under age, Lady Caroline's dress allowance and certain payments after she became Lady Ancram, a few payments for her son and daughter, liveries for his indoor servants, breeches, caps and smocks for the stablemen, shoes for all servants, and that hidden, unknown sum which went on materials for household use. The amount spent on himself can only be guessed—possibly it was something over £250 a year.

Fitzwalter's accounts provide useful source material for the local historian, for those interested in London's topographical and social history. For instance, they add a little to the accumulated knowledge of London tradesmen in early Georgian times and particularly those who supplied clothing. Over 50 names are recorded; these deserve some comment.

Tailors

In the 1720s and 1730s, Nicholas Scott was Fitzwalter's tailor. He would present a running account about twice a year, and Fitzwalter would pay off £100 from time to time. Then, in 1736, he cleared off the arrears (£415 16s. 6d.) and decided to pay in full as bills were presented to him.

In the late 1730s and early 1740s, his tailor was Henry Joseph La Motte, who became "lately deceased" in December 1744, when Fitzwalter paid his widow £143 in settlement of all accounts. Then he patronised the Wilmson family until some time before March 1747, when William Davies, John Wilmson's executor and, presumably, his partner, became the head of the firm. Davies remained his principal tailor for at least as long as Fitzwalter continued to keep accounts.

Probably, throughout the period 1724–54, Fitzwalter spent about £44 a year for his own tailored clothes and perhaps a little less on servants' liveries.

Breeches Makers

Several names occur—
How, 1725
Cheeseborough, Joseph, 1729–31
Plafor, Samuel, 1735–7
Lee, Thomas, 1738–46
Barker, William, 1749–53

Most breeches were ordered for Fitzwalter's livery and stable servants, at the rate of roughly one new pair per servant every two years. The cost was nearly always a guinea a pair. Occasionally, Fitzwalter ordered a pair for Lord Holderness.

Hosiers

Fitzwalter patronised a number of hosiers; those named were—
Harrison & Townshead (later, 1738, Townshead & Holford), Golden Fleece, Cheapside, 1726–40
Hawson, William (later, Anne H.), 1732–44
Fryer (or Friard), Augustus, 1748–51
Smith, Edward, 1730–50, mainly for livery stockings
Downes, —, in the Strand, 1725–9.

There was little variation in the price of stockings—
black silk, 14s.–18s.
grey silk, 15s.–£1 1s.
worsted, 4s. 8d.–6s. 6d.
thread, 3s.–4s.
worsted under-stockings, 5 pairs for 14s.
livery stockings, 5s.

Excluding possible purchases at Bath and Tunbridge Wells, Fitzwalter spent about £7–£8 a year, including livery stockings.

Woollen Drapers

Early on, 1725–27, Shelly & Longley were his woollen drapers, Later, he dealt mainly but not exclusively with Galfridus Mann "at the Blackmore's Head in the Strand". His total expenditure for the years 1730–53 was £1,867 8s. 2d., an annual average of £98 5s. 7d. It is frequently impossible to distinguish between goods used for clothing and goods for household use.

Linen Drapers
Five names are given
    Chamier, Mlle., 1725–36. She also supplied lace
    Campion, —, Jermyn Street, 1737–39
    Wand, Elizabeth, 1737
    Desoret, Mrs., 1742–3
    Stephenson, —, 1744
The annual average spent with Mlle. Chamier was £25–£26, but it is clear that Fitzwalter forgot to record a number of payments.

Mercers
Fitzwalter dealt almost exclusively at one shop—Mrs. Vicars (then John V., *d.* 1746/7; then, H. Parsons), 1728–54, at the Black Lion, King Street, Covent Garden. His entries are defective, but the average annual expenditure was between £54 and £59.

Lace men
Six names are recorded—
    Hicks, —., 1726
    de Vlieger, Mrs., 1725–7
    Chamier, Mlle., 1725–36 (*see also,* Linen drapers)
    Alexander, —., *c.* 1734
    Smart, H., *c.* 1735, especially gold and silver lace
    Basnet, William (after 1744, Basnet and Newton), 1731–54.
        W.B. *d.* 1754
Again, the entries are defective, for instance, Fitzwalter's payments to Basnet averaged £23–£24 annually, but the true average could be as high as £32.

Hatters
Fitzwalter dealt occasionally with Mr. Allan, 1725, and Mrs. (later, Robert) Oliphant, 1737–53, and he bought plush caps for his postillion from Lucas; but his main hatter was Melchior (later, Anthony) Wagner, Pall Mall. Over the years, 1726–54, he spent £243 11s. 7d. with Wagner, an annual average of 8 guineas, the greater part of it for servants' hats.

Glovers
The glovers are not always named. Claude Dubois seems to have been his chief supplier during the years 1732–43. James Dalvy's name occurs in 1746. Gloves were usually 2s. a pair.

Wigmakers

No fewer than nine names are recorded—
Robinet, —, 1725–6
Protein (once given as Poitevin) Noel, in Leicester Fields, 1728–31
Bonet, —, Covent Garden, 1729–35
Mertens, Henry, a German, 1732-35
Fromantel, Charles (*see* Miscellaneous)
Mathieu (Matthew) Stephen, 1733–41
Jardins, Gabriel des, 1741–2
Houghton, William, 1743–53
Fryard, Augustus, 1749–51

A bob wig cost £3 up to 1733; then, usually, £3 3s. or £3 13s. 6d.; one entry at £4 4s. No bob wigs recorded before 1729. A tied wig cost between £6 and 7 guineas on average. Fitzwalter bought one tied wig and one bob wig per year.

Shoemakers

Seven names are given—
Bagnol, —, 1725
Fisher, Benjamin, 1729–32
Clement, —, 1730
Sheppard, Henry, Pall Mall, 1734–38. Mainly for Lord Holderness
Tull, —, 1738
Bryer, James, 1740–47. Mainly for livery shoes
Garner, "a Quaker", "in Westminster", 1728–30
Smit, —, a German, 1748

The payments do not usually distinguish between Fitzwalter's own shoes and those of his servants; maybe, he bought no more than a pair a year for himself. But he paid Henry Sheppard £8 11s. 6d. for 23 pairs of shoes and pumps for Lord Holderness for the period, Jan. 1734 to Dec. 1735. Ordinary shoes cost 6s.–8s., but one pair, specifically for Fitzwalter himself, cost a guinea. "String" shoes were 8s., "shamy" shoes, 10s.; slippers, 9s.; boots for the postillion, 10s.; and half-jack boots were £1 10s.

Miscellaneous

It is difficult to assign definite trades to some shopkeepers; for instance, Mademoiselle Chamier (see earlier) sold lace and she was also a linen draper. Mrs. Barnes (later, Miles Barnes), 1726–33, sold muslin cravats at 6s. and holland for shirts at 10s. a yard. Cutler, who supplied Fitzwalter over a long period, 1734–52, sold snuff handkerchiefs and India handkerchiefs at 4s. 6d. and night cravats at 5s., but he also supplied muffs! Charles de Fromantell, 1733–47, mainly sold wigs, but on November 13th, 1733, Fitzwalter "bot. of one De Fromantell 2yds ½ of a Rich Brocade of French stuff, on a Green Velvet ground, for the marriage of the Princess Royal w(i)th the Prince of Orange, £16 16s." Mrs. Anna Dupuis, 1738–54, called herself a milliner, but she sold a variety of clothes including holland shirts for Fitzwalter and frocks for little Lady Louisa Kerr.

Clothing—selective extracts

		£	s.	d.
1725	Feb. 17th			
	To Mrs. De Vlieger in part of her bill of £83 for lace, etc.	50	0	0
	22nd			
	To silver galloon &c for eight servants hats for liveries	2	8	6
	Mar. 13th			
	To Mr. Robinet, perriwig maker, in full for one tied wig	7	0	0
	Apr. 7th			
	To Mr. Vicars for a mourning night gown for myself, £5 10s., and for mourning for Mrs. Vicars and Mrs. Jones, £11 ...	16	10	0
	9th			
	To Madamoiselle Chamier pd. a bill for two pair of laced ruffs for myself, and for cambrics for self and servants for mourning	20	2	0
	Nov. 13th			
	Pd. for nine pairs of shoes, for Lady Caroline, 4, for Lord Holderness, 5, at Hatfield	1	11	6

	£	s.	d.
1726 Mar. 6th			
Bt. and paid for of Mrs. Barnes's, 12 muslin cravats at 6s. each	3	12	0
17th			
To Mr. Downes in full for 6 pair of thread stockings for myself and one of silk at 19s., and cleaning two pair	2	4	0
May 3rd			
To Mr. Scot, my tailor, for a piece of India dimity to make me 3 waistcoats and Lord Holderness, 2	4	5	0
14th			
To Lady Holderness, bills for making Lady Caroline's clothes, and for little Schomberg	8	1	0
Dec. 19th			
To Mr. Hicks, laceman, in full for gold and silver lace for Lord Holderness and Lady Caroline Darcy	36	17	0
1727 Feb. 3rd			
To Mr. Shelley and Longley, woollen drapers, in full of all accounts	54	14	0
Apr. 11th			
To Mr. Scot, my tailor, in farther part of his bill of £203	100	0	0
Aug. 16th			
To Mrs. Chamier for cambric and other things for myself on the mourning for the King	13	12	6
Nov. 24th			
To Melchior Wagner, hatter, for hats for Lord Holderness, £2 13s., for my servants, £10 7s. 6d., in all and in full	13	0	6
1728 Apr. 18th			
To Mlle. Chamier's bill pd. in full for 42 ells of holland for 14 shirts for me at 10s. 6d. per ell, and for linen for mourning for all the servants in my family, pd. in full	42	14	0

	£	s.	d.

May 9th
To the Quaker shoemaker in Westminster,
viz: for a pair of leather gaiters, 18s., for
a pair of shoes, 6s. 6d.   1   4 6

July 22nd
To boots, 2 pair of shoes, 2 pair of stock-
ings for Stouton, under the groom   ...   1   7 0

Aug. 17th
To the glover for mourning gloves for
myself and servants on my brother Fitz-
water's mourning 1 14 0

Oct. 2nd
Wilkins for 3 pair of white linen stockings
to wear under my boots   1   3 0

Nov. 29th
To Mrs. Vicars, mercer, for 14 yds and a
half of black velvet at 25s. per yd. for a
suit of clothes, with a shagreen silk lining   21 10 0

1729 Feb. 6th
To my Lady Fitzwalter for 8 handkerchiefs
she bought for me, &c 2 2 0

Mar. 21st
To Joseph Cheesborough for nine pairs of
buckskin breeches at 24s. per pair, and
one pair of leather breeches at 9s.   ...   11 5 0

Apr. 30th
To B. Fisher, shoemaker, for a pair of
half jack boots 1 10 0

June 12th
To Mr. Vicars in full for what was due
from me on account of Lady Caroline,
myself, or mourning for my servants on
account of my brother's mourning or the
late King's 100 0 0

Nov. 12th
Pd. Mons. Protein in full for a bob, who at
the same time brought me home a tied
wig, not pd. for 3 3 0

		£	s.	d.
Dec. 12th				
Pd. Mr. Scott, my tailor, in full for 5 yds. of olive-coloured cloth, which he bought for me, and is trimmed with gold		4	7	6
26th				
To Bonet, the perriwig-maker in Covent Garden, for a tied wig		8	8	0
1730 Apr. 20th				
To John Clement, shoemaker (who never fitted me), his bill in full, 4 pairs of shoes		1	10	0
May 20th				
Pd. Townshead, the hosier at the Golden Fleece in Cheapside, in full his bill ...		5	6	0
Aug. 11th				
Bought 6 nightcaps, 12s. & petty expenses			17	0
Dec. 8th				
Pd. Mr. Wagner, the hatter, for ten hats for livery servants with gold lace, for the first of March, 1729/30, and for one hat for myself, and in full of all accounts ...		10	9	0
1731 Feb. 12th				
Pd. Mr. Scot, my tailor, in part of an old bill of which there remains due to him, £162, so that now there remains due to him on this bill, £100 being now pd., only £62		100	0	0
Mar. 6th				
To Edmund Smith for 9 pair of grey stockings for the livery servants for the last Birthday, being the 1st of March ...		2	5	0
9th				
Joseph Cheesborough in Windmill Street for nine pair of leather breeches for the livery servants, March 1st, 1730(/31) ...		9	9	0
May 26th				
Pd. William Basnet, laceman, in part of a bill of £79		25	4	0

		£	s.	d.
Dec. 31st				
To Thos. Brown for altering my baron's robes to an earl's. Pd. this day		6	8	6
1732 Jan. 1st				
To John Harrison, Golden Fleece, Cheapside, in full for stockings		4	2	1
Feb. 8th				
To Monsr. Noel Protein, perriwig maker, for one bob wig, £3, & for one tied wig, £7, and in full		10	0	0
16th				
Pd. Mr. Day, £50 on account, and in part of a bill delivered in for cloth for one year, of £98 9s. 5d.		50	0	0
May 10th				
Pd. — Dubois for 6 pair of gloves, 12s. Pd. also William Hawson his bill in full for stockings £3 15s.		4	7	0
June 2nd				
Pd. Henry Mertens, German perriwigmaker, in full for a tied wig		6	6	0
Aug. 12th				
Pd. Adam Dryden, a staymaker for Lady Caroline Darcy, an old bill due before her allowance		3	8	6
Pd. Mrs. Ward, linen draper, in full to July 21st last past		14	14	3¾
1733 Jan. 9th				
Pd. Barnes and Mrs. Smith in the City a bill for muslin cravats &c, and in full of all demands		5	18	3
May 31st				
Pd. Peter Lucas for a blue velvet cap for the morning			16	0
June 2nd				
Pd. my Lady Caroline Darcy her half year's allowance for her clothes, due the 26th of May last, £50, and, also £25 for a suit of clothes for the Queen's Birthday the 1st of March last		75	0	0

		£	s.	d.
June 16th				
Pd. Mr. Scot, tailor, in full satisfaction of a bill or bills delivered in, ending 1726/7, with also a bill due on my brother's account, having pd. him before, £535, the said bill amounting to £594 16s. 3½d. pd. him this day in full of the sd. bill the sum of £59, and is in full of sd. bill		59	0	0
Pd. Mr. Scott, tailor, the sum of £200 on account of a bill delivered in a few days since amounting to £411 19s. 2½d. ...		200	0	0
23rd				
Pd. Johnson for three caps of black for the groom, the stableboy and the postillion, 6s. apiece			18	0
Sept. 4th				
To Mr. Scot, the tailor, for two yds. one quarter and nail of black velvet for a pair of breeches at £1 3s. per yd.		2	12	0
1734 Jan. 12th				
Pd. Mr. Alexander, laceman, his bill in full for silver tassels for my Lady Caroline Darcy		2	10	0
Mar. 12th				
Pd. Mr. Cutler for 14 snuff handkerchiefs		3	3	0
Aug. 1st				
Pd. Mr. Mann, woollen draper, by the hands of Mr. Markland the sum of fifty pounds six shillings, which is in full of a bill delivered in of £130 6s. 1d., of which I had paid £80 before, which bill come down Jan. 1733		50	6	0
1735 Jan. 13				
Pd. Mr. H. Smart, laceman, for a broad silver trimming, &c, for my Lady Caroline's petticoat when she held up the train of the Princess Royal at her marriage with the Prince of Orange, March, 1733/4		75	17	6

	£	s.	d.

Nov. 17th

Pd. Mr. Basnet, laceman, for a white silk waistcoat, flowered and embroidered with gold for the Earl of Holderness for my (*Lady*) Ancram's wedding   16   16   0 -

1736   Feb. 13th

Pd. Mr. Shephard, shoemaker in Pall-Mall, his bill for shoes for the Earl of Holderness in full from Jan. 6th, 1735 to Dec. 18th, 1735, being for 23 pair of shoes and pumps   8   11   6

Feb. 14th

Pd. Mr. Nicholas Scot, tailor, the sum of four hundred and four pounds, sixteen shillings in full satisfaction for two bills delivered in for making clothes for myself and liveries for my servants, and for things bought by him for me, and also a little bill of eleven pounds and sixpence, and in full of all demands to this day ...   415   16   6

Apr. 3rd

Pd. Mr. Galfridus Mann, woollen draper in the Strand, his bill in full for one year ending Jan. 8th, 1735/6 for myself and Lord Holderness   91   16   11

Oct. 23rd

Pd. Mlle. Chamier her bill in full for linen for the house and for my own wearing, from March 4th, 1734/35   81   3   3

Pd. at the same time to Mlle. Chamier a bill for wearing linen for the Earl of Holderness from Oct. 8th, 1735. Pd. in full   ...   22   13   0

Nov. 26th

Pd. Mrs. Jones, my wife's woman, a bill for making shirts, handkerchiefs, &c, for my Lord Holderness   3   12   0

Dec. 8th

Pd. Alex. Hume for a pair of boots for the Earl of Holderness for the riding-house, & in full   1   5   0

	£	s.	d.

1737 May 28th
Pd. Mr. Oliphant, hatter, for a hat for myself 16 0

June 10th
Pd. Mrs. Jones, my wife's woman, for cambric and holland for necking, wrist-banding and ruffling 14 shirts, cambric at 13s. per yd. and holland at 10s. per ell, for my Lord Holderness 4 8 3

Nov. 3rd
Pd. Mr. Vicars, mercer at the Black Lion in Covent Garden, the remainder of his bill of £226 in full, having pd. him £100 before, and is in full of my bills to May 24th last 126 14 0

1738 Jan. 10th
Pd. to Claude Johnson the sum of £24 12s. for the use of Mr. James Lowdoun & Co., merchants of Glasgow, for 61 yards of linen for shirts at 8s. per yd., which is 10s. per ell, said linen cloth made there, and is in full of all accounts due to said Lowdoun and Co. N.B. 16 shirts were made for me out of this linen, Nov. and Dec. 1737 ... ...   24 12 0

Oct. 30th
Pd. Mr. Cutler for one dozen of India handkerchiefs, and in full 2 12 0

1739 June 21
Pd. Galfridus Mann, woollen draper at the Blackmoor's Head in the Strand, his two bills in full for myself and the Earl of Holderness to Christmas, 1738, for myself and liveries 175 17 0

Sept. 29
Pd.—Shephard, shoemaker, his bill in full of all accounts, thin shoes at 7s. and strong ones at 8s. per pair 3 9 0

	£	s.	d.

Nov. 16

Gave my Lady Ancram an embroidered apron, cost 1 **15** 0

1740 Jan. 8

Pd. Steph. Mathieu for 2 bob wigs, viz., June 1st and Aug. 20th, 1739, and in full of all accounts 7 7 0

Mar. 8

Pd. Armstrong Jones for one pair of silk and 2 pair of worsted stockings, and in full of all accounts 1 8 6

May 8

Pd. James Bryer, shoemaker, his bill in full for one pair of boots for my postillion, 18s., and for four pair of shoes for myself   2 7 0

Oct. 20

Pd. my Lord Ancram for a great white new market coat he procured for me 3 6 0

1741 Feb. 11

Pd. Richardson, a Scots' tailor, a bill pretended to be due from my brother, Fitzwalter, Jan. 1728. N.B. I take it all to be a cheat. However, I pd. it in full ...   3 13 6

Feb. 21

Pd. Mr. La Motte, tailor his bill for making clothes from Jan. 10th, 1739/40 to Dec. 18th, 1740, £47 15s. Pd. him at the same time his bill for making my servants' liveries from June 3rd, 1740 to Nov. 20th, 1740, the sum of £39 7s. 6d., which is in full of all accounts to this day 87 2 6

Apr. 27

Pd. Gabriel des Jardins for a tied perriwig   5 5 0

May 18

Pd. Mr. Lynch, tailor, his bill for making my Lord Newbattle a suit of clothes, and materials, in full 2 19 0

		£	s.	d.
Nov. 25				
Gave Frederick, Mr. La Motte's head man, on fitting on my Birthday clothes ...		1	1	0
1742 Mar. 30				
Pd. Mr. Oliphant, hatter, for a hat, feather and gold lace for my Lord Newbattle, £1 8s. 6d., and for a hat for myself, 16s., in full of all accounts		2	4	6
Apr. 10				
Pd. Anthony Wagner, my hatter, for a hat for myself, 18s., and for a black girdle and buckle		1	3	0
July 17				
Pd. Mr. Yeo, hosier, for 2 pair of dyed white silk hose		1	15	0
Dec. 6				
Pd. Mr. — Cutler for 13 red handkerchiefs, and in full		2	12	0
1743 Jan. 8				
Pd. Anne Hawson for 2 pair of dice white silk stockings		1	18	0
Mar. 2				
Pd. Claude Dubois for 12 pair of gloves, and in full		1	4	0
Apr. 20				
Pd. Mr. Cutler for a Turkish-red silk for outside of a night gown		3	3	0
Dec. 19				
Pd. William Milliard in full for 2 working frocks			15	0
1744 Mar. 17				
Pd. Mr. Newton, partner to Mr. Basnet, lace man, on account of a bill delivered in of £148 8s. 5d.		80	0	0
May 18				
Pd. Mrs. Dupuis a bill of shirts, &c., for myself, and in full of said, but there rests another due. Pd.		34	13	0

	£	s.	d.

Oct. 31

Gave Mr. Leigh to buy him clothes, going now on board one of the King's ships (as he says) to the West Indies 5 5 0

Dec. 11

Pd. Mrs. Winifrid La Motte, widow and administratrix of Henry Joseph La Motte, tailor, lately deceased, in full of all accounts due either to her late husband or herself 143 0 0

1745 May 14

Pd. John Wilmson, my tailor, in full for Lord Newbattle and for a pair of knit breeches and 2 cotton waistcoats for myself 7 1 0

Oct. 28

Pd.—Pow for a pair of boots for my postillion 15 0

1746 Mar. 4

Pd. James Dalvy for one dozen of white gloves, and in full 1 1 0

Mar. 13

Pd.—Wilmson, my tailor, his bill for velvet for breeches and for red cloth for a waist-coat 3 11 10½

Mar. 15

Pd. Mr. Yeo in Old Bond Street (for) a pair of black silk stockings, and in full ... 14 0

Mar. 31

Pd. Mr. G. Mann, woollen draper, his bill in full to Michaelmas, 1745 ... ... 98 1 0

July 1

Pd. John Wilmson, my tailor, his bill for six white India dimity waistcoats ... 5 17 0

1747 Feb. 16

Pd. Mr. John Riding, sole executor of Mr. John Vicars, mercer, deceased, the sum of £100, which is in full of Mr. Vicars' bill of £258 19s., having pd. before to said Riding £158 19s. 100 0 0

	£	s.	d.

Mar. 30
Pd.—Davies by power (*of*) attorney from executrix of John Wilmson, tailor, deceased, on account of a bill of £92 7s. 6½d., delivered, £21. Rests due £71 7s. 6½d. **21 0 0**

June 4
Pd. Mr. William Davies, my tailor, on account of his bill of £57 17s. 4d. delivered in, £40 ... ... **40 0 0**

June 17
Pd. Dixon, my cook, for 11 Milan handkerchiefs **3 6 0**

Sept. 15
Pd. for 2 yds. and ½ of red shag for breeches bought of Thos. and Francis Caryl at the Wheatsheaf in the Strand **1 15 0**

1748 Mar. 3
Pd. Henry Parsons, linen draper, on account of his bill of £85 7s. **45 0 0**

Mar. 21
Pd. Smitz, a German shoemaker, for a pair of shoes, 7s. 6d., and for one great shoe, 4s. **11 6**

May 16
Pd. Mr. Houghton, perriwig maker, for a tied wig, and in full **6 6 0**

May 23
Pd. Mr. Robert Oliphant and son their bill in full for servants' hats **14 5 0**

1749 Feb. 27
Pd. Mr. William Davies, my Tailor, his bill in full for things bought by him for me, and for all frock and livery cloth for my servants for the year 1749(?1748) ... **72 10 0**

May 2
Pd. Augustus Fryard for a tied perriwig, and in full **8 8 0**

		£	s.	d.
1750	Jan. 13			
	Pd. William Barker for 9 pair of leather breeches for all my livery servants in Town, all just brought here, and in full	9	9	0
1751	Sept. 13			
	Pd. Richard Harford of Bath for 32 yds. ¾ of cloth for frocks for my livery servants, at 8s. 3d. per yd., and in full	13	1	0
	Sept. 23			
	Pd. Mrs. Jones all her bills in full for mourning for herself, for my housekeeper and for 2 maidservants, (*Lady Fitzwalter d. 7 Aug., '51*)	46	6	8
	Nov. 26			
	Pd. John Cartwright in full for Chamois shoes for five servants out of livery ...	2	5	0
1752	Apr. 24			
	Pd. Charles Reak, Lady Louisa's shoemaker in full	3	4	0
	Apr. 28			
	Pd. Mrs. Dupuis in full for frocks for my Lady Louisa	9	2	8
1753	Aug. 8			
	Pd. Mr. Basnet for gold and silver twist for Lady Louisa		17	0
	Oct. 1			
	Pd. Mr. Hinchliffe for 11 yds. of green tabby for my Lady Louisa, 9s. per yd., and in full	4	19	0
	Nov. 19			
	Pd. Mr. Harford of Bath his bill in full for frock and blue livery cloth. N.B. Blue cloth not good	20	2	0
	Dec. 5			
	Pd. Edwd. Farley of Cambridge Street for 21 yds. of coarse cloth, and in full ...	1	1	0
1754	Feb. 27			
	Pd. Mr. Wagner, my hatter, his bill in full for Louisa and myself	2	13	6

Oct. 17   £ s. d.
Pd. Mr. Basnet and Newton, lacemen, their
  bill in full and of all demands. Mr. Basnet
  deceased 112 1 10

Accessories

Fitzwalter's payments for accessories call for little comment. He bought a muff in December 1741 and another in March 1747. It is also interesting to note that he patronized the well-known Pinchbeck family at their shop in Fleet Street.

Accessories—selective extracts

		£	s.	d.
1726	Dec. 10			
	To Mr. Shyrack, jeweller, for setting my ruby ring and my green ring	2	2	0
1727	June 20			
	To a mourning sword, buckles, belt & other things	1	6	0
1729	Feb. 24			
	For a pair of silver shoe buckles and a silver stock-buckle	1	1	0
	May 27			
	To Mr. Chenevix at the toy shop in Pall Mall for a long gold head for a cane, with my coronet upon it	6	11	0
1730	Oct. 19			
	Pd. Mr. Grey, watchmaker, in full for the exchange of a gold watch for another ...	12	12	0
1731	Mar. 8			
	A pair of silver buckles for Lord Holderness		10	0
1732	Dec. 21			
	Pd. Pinchbeck in Fleet Street for a metal snuff-box	1	11	6
1733	June 18			
	For the exchange of the gold chain of my watch for a new one. Mr. Grey	4	4	0

		£	s.	d.
Sept. 4				
For a reed cane with a black head and spying-glass			15	0
Sept. 6				
To Monsr. Le Temps for a snuff-box ...		1	15	0
1735 Jan. 29				
To Mr. Cutler for a French ivory toothpick case			10	6
Apr. 19				
Pd. Pinchbeck in Fleet Street for a pair of shoe and knee buckles, 15s., and for a head to a cane, 10s. 6d.		1	5	6
Apr. 24				
For a new dial plate put to my gold watch by Monsr. Martineau in Orange Street ...			16	0
1736 Feb. 21				
Pd. Phillipe Fouache for a black tortoise-shell wrought onion snuff-box in gold...		4	14	0
Mar. 12				
Pd. Phillipe Fouache for a tortoiseshell onion snuff-box set in gold		5	5	0
1737 Nov. 15				
Changed away an old pair of little gold sleeve buttons for a larger pair, of Mrs. Chenevix; difference			19	0
1740 May 7				
Pd. Benjamin Grey, watchmaker, his bill in full to Jan. 10th, 1738		11	6	6
Nov. 26				
To Fleureau, sword cutler, for a buckle for my belt having a new silver clasp, 16s., and steel buckles, &c.		1	0	0
1741 Feb. 9				
To Mr. Deards for a cane with a little gold head with my crest upon it, and in full...		5	15	6
1742 May 13				
Pd. Mr. Sharvel for a gold repeating watch, in money, £41, and by an old gold watch of my own, valued £12		53	0	0

		£	s	d.
1744	Jan. 23			
	Pd. B. Grey, watchmaker, in full to Christmas, 1743	3	19	0
1745	Mar. 1			
	Pd. Mr. Sharvel for cleaning my watch ...		12	0
1746	Mar. 5			
	Pd. Mr. Cutler for a muff in full	2	2	0
1747	Feb. 12			
	Pd. T. Young for Mr. Eymaker for setting my Scotch pebble ring given me by the Earl of Ancram	1	1	0
1749	Dec. 15			
	Pd. Mrs. Chenevix for silver shoe buckles for my Lord Newbattle	1	1	0
1751	Nov. 18			
	Pd. Signor Bernardo for 2 razors	1	1	0
	Dec. 16			
	Pd. Mr. Sharvel for fitting up a gold watch I gave my Lady Louisa Kerr	3	13	6
1753	Jan. 3			
	Pd. Mr. Grey for a gold chain for Louisa's watch	5	5	0
	Jan. 11			
	Pd. Mr. Grey and partner for a shagreen watch case for my Lady Louisa	1	1	0

CHAPTER FIVE

PERSONAL TRANSPORT

Future research may well reveal that personal transport from Royal Daimlers back to Boadicea's chariot has always been costly; certainly it was for Fitzwalter, that most parsimonious peer. His aim was always to maintain his *port*. He would pay adequately to achieve this, though not always readily; and if he thought he was being overcharged, he would immediately query the cost.

An analysis of his expenditure over the ten years, 1731–40, shows that on an average his transport cost him as much as £360 annually. Even this figure may be too low: it is clear, for instance, that he did not always remember to enter his coachman's bills, which were probably over 40% higher than the *recorded* totals. Moreover, there is that frustrating element present in all accounts —the composite entry which cannot be broken down into its components.

Fitzwalter kept a coachman, a "helper" or second coachman, a groom, a postillion and a stable-boy. The groom, Edward Smith (wages, £6 a year), was with Fitzwalter from 1724, the beginning of the account book series, to 1736, or even later. He accompanied Fitzwalter on long journeys and, presumably, when his master went from the Pall Mall house to Moulsham and *vice-versa*; otherwise he seems to have been based at Moulsham Hall, as was certainly the stable-boy (wages, £3 a year). The two coachmen did not live in; they were given board wages of seven shillings a week; the second coachman was paid £5–£6 a year. Fitzwalter's first postillion, Ned Stouton, and his brother, were serving their master back in the old Hertfordshire days, before Fitzwalter acquired Moulsham Hall. Ned's wages were £4 a year, rising to £5 in 1735—when Fitzwalter remembered to pay him! Maybe he lived in—there were probably a few quiet, insignificant corners in Schomberg House and Moulsham Hall. He and the 2nd coachman were carried off by smallpox early in 1740; Fitzwalter noted, characteristically, that it cost him rather more to bury poor Ned than he owed him in wages!

Apart from Ned, postillions and second coachmen came and went —theirs were not permanent posts for anybody with ambition. The coachman's position was different; the job was a hard one, but one of the most lucrative in the servant class. Fitzwalter's coachman in 1724 was Matthew Jackson. His annual wage was £5, and he made another £5 oiling, greasing and clouting the coaches. He left in December 1726, and was succeeded by Thomas Bedell, whose annual wage was probably £7. He was dismissed in November 1727 "for cheating me at the Bath"—on Fitzwalter's first recorded visit to that Spa. The next coachman, Thomas Garnham, stayed throughout the remaining period of the account-books. He was paid £10 a year in wages; he got £6 a year for greasing and clouting the coaches. Then, from 1736, he was paid £15 annually "for shoeing, physicing and all sort of farrier's work for seven coach horses". For the saddle horses and, presumably, all horses on the home farm at Moulsham, Fitzwalter continued to patronise local smiths.

Fitzwalter usually kept 7 or 8 coach horses, and perhaps usually 2 and never more than 5 saddle horses; it was easy to hire extra horses when needed and much more economical—horses were expensive to feed. The corn chandler's bills averaged over £37 a year; the coachman's bills may have averaged £65. Usually, the account book entries of the coachman's bills give no details, but occasionally (see extracts) the amounts and cost of hay are given— one actual bill (loose in one of the account books) has survived

"1751 Sept. 15	£	s.	d.
Load of hay	2	6	0
Half a load of straw		9	0
Pound of soap			6
Paid the turnpike 5 times			10
Grinding the scissors			6
and end Sept. 29	2	16	10

"Received Sept. 29, 1751, of the Right Honourable the
Earl Fitzwalter the sum of Two Pound, Sixteen
Shillings and Ten Pence, in full of this bill p(er)
Tho. Garnham."

Schomberg House in Pall Mall had no mews; it was divided from
the grounds of Marlborough House only by a narrow lane; thus,
Fitzwalter had to rent stable accommodation. From 1724 (maybe
earlier) to 1741, he patronised Jonathan Healy, stable-keeper, of
Little Queen's Street, Golden Square. The rent rose from £29 to
£32 in 1727 for a seven-horse stable and standing for three coaches,
and then to £36 when Fitzwalter needed accommodation for
another coach horse. It went back to £32 when he reduced his
coaches from three to two. Then, in 1741, he changed to a ten-
horse stable (rent £34) off Jermyn Street, belonging to Robert Mell.
This was a saving in charges for stabling saddle horses; indeed,
Fitzwalter may rarely have had more than two saddle horses of his
own in Town at any one time, and he could now stable them with
his coach horses.

Horses, especially coach horses, were expensive, although prices
remained steady throughout the period of the account books.
Between 1731 and 1740 he bought 12 coach horses at an average
price of £26 6s. 0d.; his average annual expenditure for that period
was £30 7s. 0d. During the same period he bought 11 more horses,
mainly hacks. He was always present, with Garnham his coachman,
when a horse was bought. If the vendor gave Garnham half a
guinea, Fitzwalter would give the same amount to the vendor's
servant. He did not like it when Mr. Thomas Petre raised the rate

"1730   Feb. 20
           To Mr. Thomas Petre of Fidler's for a pair of stoned
           coach horses with blazes, one 8-year old, the other
           seven this grass—£42 0s. 0d.

   To Mr. Petre's servant, as he gave to mine, £1 1s. 0d."

He owned more than one chaise—he mentions them occasionally. It is almost certain that they were always kept at Moulsham.
But it is in his coaches, however, that he took such a great interest.
He called them by different names from time to time, according to
fashion and his own fancy—travelling coach, berlin, chariot,
landau, "lemosyne". His first coach builder was a William Grimes;
then, from 1728 to 1748, he patronised William Robins. He kept a

running account with Robins, but if Fitzwalter ordered anything special, Robins would render a separate account, which Fitzwalter would settle—fairly promptly. In 1749 he went over to a Samuel Butler, and continued to deal with him until he ceased to keep accounts. Butler kept his equipage up to date—he built a new landau and a new chariot. But in 1752, Fitzwalter forgot to pay his excise duty on them, not for the first time. The original reminder has been preserved, loose, in the account book. It was not sent to Fitzwalter until over 8 months later, and it is couched in a style which could serve as a model to modern bureaucrats—"My Lord, As the payment of your Coach Duty may have slipped your memory, therefore permit me to remind you that your last Year's Payment determined 26th Day, March, 1751."

Personal Transport—selective extracts

		£	s.	d.
1725	Sept. 25			
	Pd. Molineaux the wheeler a bill in full of £12, having pd. £6 before. Remains due for a set of chaise wheels, £5 5s. 0d. ...	6	0	0
1727	May 5			
	Pd. to a jockey in Bishopsgate Street for a black, stoned coach horse, with a white streak in his face, four years old, in money, sixteen pounds, and a coach horse of mine, with a blaze in his face, by way of exchange. His servant could not write; the witnesses that I pd. the sixteen pounds were Wilkins and Johnson, my serv(*an*)ts	16	0	0
	June 13			
	To Hooke, bit maker in the mews, for 6 new bits for the travelling harness, £2 5s. 0d., for one saddle-bit, 7s. 0d., and for bosses and tinning 2 town bits &ca	3	3	6
	June 26			
	To Bryan Payne, corn chandler, bill being £29 16s. 0d. for Christmas to Midsummer, paid in part £20 0s. 0d.	20	0	0

To the R.t Hon.ble the Earl of Fitzwalter

My Lord

AS the Payment of your Coach Duty may have flipt your Memory, therefore permit me to remind you, that your last Year's Payment determined 26 th Day March 175 1

Excise Office London

John Drop's

		£	s.	d.
July 21				
To William Dissel, coach painter, in full of his bill of £36 0s. 0d.		20	0	0
Nov. 6				
Spent in my journey to and from the Bath, with a coach and six horses, and 7 saddle horses		24	0	0
Nov. 6				
To the carriage by the waggon to and from Bath		7	4	0
Nov. 14				
To Thos. Bedell, my coachman, who I have this day discharged for cheating me at the Bath, in full of yearly wages, £6 8s. 0d., to the oiling and greasing the coach and harness, £5 9s. 10d., for board and wages in full, 7s. 0d., in all		12	2	10
1728 Dec. 9				
To Mr. Robins, my coachmaker, a bill for putting my coach and chariot in mourning,* £30, and for furbishing up and painting my chaise, £9 12s. 0d. Total ...		39	12	0
1729 Jan. 18				
To Mr. Young, my farrier, in full for one year for shoeing, &ca. ending Christmas last, for 7 coach horses, £18 0s. 0d., and for extras, £3 11s. 0d.		21	11	0
1730 April 23				
Pd. Mr. Healy, stable-keeper, in full for one year's rent and in full to Christmas, 1729, for an eight-horse stable and coach-house. N.B. from last Christmas I am to pay for another coach-house at £4 per year, rent		32	0	0
Nov. 24				
Pd. Edward Smith the groom a bill for turnpikes, &ca		1	1	8

* For his brother, Charles, 18th Lord Fitzwalter.

Dec. 31   £   s.   d.
>   Pd. Thos. Garnham, my coachman, for one
>   year's clouting and greasing, £6 0s. 0d.,
>   and also his bill for hay, straw, &ca, in
>   full to the 24th inst. and also for five
>   white frocks for both stables at 6s. per
>   frock   14   0   9

1731 July 23
>   Pd. at the White Hart in Whitechapel for
>   5 horses standing 6 nights 1 16   0

Dec. 24
>   To Monsr. (*Paul*) de Lamerie for a grey
>   gelding, coming six, belonging to Col. Van
>   Thuine 18 18   0

1732 Jan. 18
>   To Martha Bradford, sadler, bot. and paid
>   for this day, 7 Dutch collars, 6 curry-
>   combs, 6 brushes, 6 cotton rubbing-cloths
>   bound, 4 whisk brushes, 2 hair cloths, 4
>   water brushes, 2 inside ditto, 2 cards, 4
>   hempen halters, a mare comb, a large
>   sponge 5 12   8

June 1
>   Pd. John Lynn, stable-keeper at the Rose &
>   Crown at Hyde Park Corner, for the
>   standing of my grey horse and my Lord
>   Holderness's horse at livery, one from the
>   2nd of April, the other from the 8th of
>   May 5 12   6

June 16
>   My grey mare was this day leaped by Mr.
>   Alcorne's chestnut horse for the last time,
>   she having been leaped twice the 9th inst.
>   by the same horse, but the last time I
>   think is most likely to stand. To Mr.
>   Alcorne for his chestnut horse leaping my
>   grey mare this day   1   1   0

		£	s	d.
1733 Aug. 28				
Pd. Geo. Vaughan for a new chair lined with blue caffay for my Lady Fitzwalter in part of his bill of		15	15	0
Sept. 17				
Pd. Barker the wheelwright on acco(un)t this day given in of £13 4s. 2d.		5	5	0
1734 June 7				
Pd. Mr. Wood, stable-keeper in Marlborough Mews, for the hire of a coach horse for 19 days, & in full		3	16	0

July 20

I set out for Oxford this day with my Lady Fitzwalter, my Lady Caroline Darcy and my Lord Holderness in order to see that place and Blenheim House.

July 25

We returned this day to London by way of Windsor from our Oxford expedition. I had five saddle-horses and six coach horses and spent in this expedition, including the hire of one coach horse, having left three lame ones at home ... 24 11 0

Aug. 19

Pd. George Lewis, collar-maker, his two bills in full, viz., the first is £4 16s. 0d., the 2nd is five pounds eleven shillings, and is in full to the tenth of this last August ... 10 7 0

Query, whether I can find an old bill of his given in of £23, of which (*he*) pretends about £4 still remains unpaid.

1735 Jan. 13

N.B. Monday Jan(ua)ry 13th, Darlow my farrier began his operations in order to cure a blood spavin on one of my coach horses. That day he took up the vein of that leg, and four days later fired that joint and laid on a blistering-strengthening-charge 3 17 6

Dec. 19   £ s d.
    To five serv(an)ts coming down in the stage
    coach, £1 5s. 0d., and expenses on the
    road for 3 of them, 5s. 6d., and for the
    other two, 3s., and for 2 hackney coaches,
    1s. 6d. 1 19 6

1736 Oct. 15
    Bought also by me during my stay at
    Knaresborough three saddle-horses of
    which two were serv(an)ts' horses. Cost   38 0 0

Dec. 6
    Pd. Mr. Robins, my coach-maker, for turn-
    ing my travelling-coach into a landau, as
    by agreement, and was brought home the
    4th of this last December 25 0 0

Dec. 6
    Pd. Robins the coach-maker also for new
    painting the landau of a mahogany colour,
    the arms remaining as they were, £4. Pd.
    him also for a new seat cloth, &ca,
    £2 5s. 0d., and for new canvas frames
    10s. Deduct for the fore-glass of the travel-
    ling-coach and other odd things, £4, so
    paid in full for all acco(un)ts for said
    landau 2 15 0

Dec. 21
    Pd. Mr. Miller, riding-master, for riding my
    sorrel colt six weeks, at 15s. per week,
    keeping included, £4 10s. 0d., for shoeing,
    2s. 6d. To Mr. Gibson, farrier, for 3
    drinks for his colt, and bleeding 5 0 6

1737 Feb. 10
    Mr. Hyde, stable-keeper, a bill delivered in of
    £47 10s. 0d. for the hire of coach horses;
    paid on acco(un)t, £26 10s. 0d. N.B. sets
    me down too many days to York and
    work when did not 26 5 0

		£	s.	d.

March 12

Pd. Thos. Garnham, my coachman, his stable bill in full for one load of hay, half a load of straw, one pound of soap and 3 pound of hog's lard, from 24th of Feb(*rua*)ry last, to the 10th of this last March 3 1 6

1738 Jan. 14

Pd. William Robins, coach-maker, in full for a complete set of six travelling-coach harness, delivered in Nov(*embe*)r last, to my use 18 0 0

Pd. William Robins, coach-maker, in full for one horse chair delivered to my use a year or two ago and now at Moulsham Hall in Essex, with the harness 16 10 0

Jan. 22

To Michael Gomery at the White Horse Inn in Whitechapel for eight horses standing 2 nights, each night, 10s. 8d., at his stable, and in full of all accounts 1 1 4

May 25

Pd. Mr. Vaughan for putting my Lady Fitzwalter's chair in mourning on the death of the late Queen 11 0 0

1739 Feb. 10

Pd. William Robins, coach-maker, in full for the use of a mourning-chariot for one year, being the time of mourning on the death of the late Queen 31 10 0

1740 March 28

Pd. John Mann, stable-keeper at the Bull in Swallow Street, for a black starred coach gelding, 15 hands, an inch and half high, coming six this grass, and in full... ... 25 0 0

April 22

Pd. William Robins, my coach-maker, his bill in full from Feb(*rua*)ry, 1728, to Jan(*uar*)y 28th, 1741, the sum of £315.

	£	s.	d.

N.B. his bill delivered in was £331 2s. 1d.,
but finding it to be very extravagant, he
agreed willingly to take as mentioned in
full satisfaction of said bill 315 0 0

1741 May 21
Pd. William Robins, coach-maker, on
account of his bill of £83 10s. 4d., viz., for
a new chariot, which came out Feb(rua)ry
19th, 1741, £84 0s. 0d., and for a new pair
of wheels to my landau, April 23rd, 1741,
£6 0s. 0d., which with other things, makes
the bill amount to £95 0s. 0d., but by
allowing for my old (chariot), £12 0s. 0d.,
reduces his bill to £83, so that there
remains due to him, £33 10s. 4d. ... 50 0 0

1742 April 1
Pd. Thomas Garnham, my coachman, the
sum of £8 15s. 0d., which is in full for half
a year's allowance, due at Lady Day, 1742,
for shoeing and medicines and all sort
of farrier's work for my seven coach
horses, from Michaelmas, 1741, which is
at the rate of fifty shillings a horse, as by
agreement for one year, ending Michaelmas, 1742 ... ... 8 15 0

1742 Nov. 22
Pd. Mr. Robert Mell, stable-keeper, one
year's rent and in full to Michaelmas,
1742, for a ten-horse stable and standing
for 2 coaches in Bothmer's Mews in
Jermyn Street 34 0 0

Pd. Robert Mell, stable-keeper, for odd
horses of mine baiting at his stable in
Bothmer's Mews, Jermyn Street 5 6

Nov. 26
N.B., forgot to be entered, pd. to Hyde,
stable-keeper in Old Bond Street, his bill

		£	s.	d.

Nov. 26th—*cont.*
for a coach and four horses I hired of him to carry serv(*ant*)ts when I went to Knaresborough, and in full of all accounts   24 10 0

1744   May 7
Pd. John Cann, a horse-dealer in Bishops-gate Street, for a black coach-gelding, four year old, with a small star and white snip, fifteen hands an inch and half high, in full 28 0 0

1745   Nov. 18
Pd. John Briggs for carrying the "limosyne" to Abingdon to my Lord Ancram in his march towards Lancashire. 3 days*   ...   1 11 6

1746   July 4
Pd. for three black plush caps for my groom, postillion and helper 1 2 6

1749   April 27
My new landau was brought home Thurs-day, April 27th, 1749, the day the grand fireworks were played off for the cele-bration of the Peace. N.B. I am to pay Mr. Butler, my coach-maker, in money, £100, and to give him my old landau, which he values at £12.

---

* Lord Ancram, husband of Fitzwalter's step-daughter, was in the dragoons who were marching to join Cumberland's army, then about to launch his campaign against Prince Charles Edward.

CHAPTER SIX

MEDICAL

The medical profession was thoroughly familiar with the golden road which led to Fitzwalter's front door. Between 1726 and 1754 he paid at least £818 on doctors' fees, £1,181 to apothecaries and £5,336 on visits to Bath and other spas. These are *recorded* payments; there are those which Fitzwalter forgot to enter and there are those missing Moulsham Hall accounts for the period, 1742–54.

As Lady Mary Wortley Montague noted, Fitzwalter had a partially paralysed arm; otherwise he suffered severely from good health, so much so that he would summon a doctor for the smallest ache or pain. In May 1740, for example, he paid an unrecorded fee to Sir Caesar Hawkins, the well-known surgeon, "for syringing both my ears, having been deaf in the left ear by a large quantity of wax for at least three weeks; by this, heard very well." In March 1748, Hawkins received five guineas "for curing my toe of a humour that had fallen into it". Sir Caesar and all Fitzwalter's London doctors were eminent practitioners; he worked them unreasonably, but they reaped their harvest of golden guineas. In the 1720s and 1730s, the famous Sir Hans Sloane was frequently called in. John Hollings, Fitzwalter's physician in the middle period of the account books, was Physician-in-Ordinary to George II, while Sir Caesar Hawkins was the King's Sergeant-Surgeon. Fitzwalter's doctors in later life, the popular Peter Shaw and the distinguished Sir John Pringle, were also Court physicians. His usual Chelmsford physician was Dr. Coe. Twelve other names are recorded but most of them were doctors called in during an emergency—Fitzwalter did not like strange doctors. His principal London apothecary was Isaac Garnier, who was succeeded by his nephew, George Garnier, but in his last years, Fitzwalter turned to John Truesdale and paid him £358 between January 1753 and December 1754. When he was at Moulsham Hall, he patronised

Abraham Griffenhoofe, the Chelmsford apothecary. Most of the £5,336 on spas was spent at Bath and Tunbridge Wells; there was one visit to Harrogate. Sometimes the products of the spas came to him; bottles of Bristol waters from the fashionable Hotwells, bottles of Pohun water from Spa, with a covering letter from his cousin and heir, Sir William Mildmay, the diplomat—"I must inform your Lordship that these waters have a different taste according to the change of wind and weather; the Pohun, for example, is flat and vapid upon the south or western wind, and is best to be drunk, say the German physicians, when the wind is northerly and the weather hot." (D/DM O1/19)

In the early years of the account books many of the professional fees were paid on behalf of the children. There was that period of hope and anxiety, the short life-span (August 1725–March 1727) of his only child, his son Schomberg (*see* chapter on "My Family"). Sir Hans Sloane and Hugh Chamberlen, member of that famous family of obstetricians, were present at the boy's birth. At first, all went well; then, from October 1726, Sir Hans and other doctors were frequently in attendance. It was during this same period that his young step-daughter, Lady Caroline Darcy, was often ill; but for the rest of her childhood the doctors collected only six guineas on her behalf. Her brother, Lord Holderness, however, seems to have been a sickly small boy and adolescent. Between 1726 and 1732 Fitzwalter paid out £48 6s. for him, and even later he was quick to call in medical advice—

> 1736   Feb. 4
>
> "To Dr. Hollings of the Earl of Holderness having a little sickness often at his stomach and breaking out with large heats and pimples upon his face, £1 1s. 0d. To Mr. Hawkins, the surgeon, for bleeding Lord Holderness, 10s. 6d."

It should also be remembered that Fitzwalter always included his servants when he referred to "my family". When they were ill he saw to it that they had proper medical attendance and nursing—

> 1740   Jan. 11
>
> "Pd. for the nurse-keeping and lodgings of Nutting my 2nd coachman during 9 days before he died of the small pox, £2 2s. 0d."

1746 Jan. 21

"Gave Mr. Hawkins, the surgeon, for Longmore my *valet de chambre,* who had a bone stuck in his throat, £1 1s. 0d."

By far the greatest part of his medical expenditure went on Lady Fitzwalter—for her gout and other complaints. Her minor ailments received the usual drastic treatment of the age. She was blistered when she had a "sort of stitch or rheumatic pains in her breast"; she was cupped when she felt giddy. Sometimes, these fits of giddiness had an interesting context. On one occasion Dr. Hollings was called to Schomberg House, "my wife having a giddiness by drinking too much Islington water the first day".

It was gout and allied diseases, however, which were Lady Fitzwalter's great enemies, and they eventually killed her. She was a sufferer before Fitzwalter married her—as Lady Mary Wortley Montague noted. In 1727, Sir Hans Sloane sent the Fitzwalters to Bath for 10 weeks, and they spent two long spells, one at Tunbridge Wells and the other at Bath, during the next four years. For another seven years the chief medical entries in the accounts refer to Fitzwalter's own little ailments; then on February 19th, 1739, there is an ominous note:

"This morning at 5 o'clock my Lady Fitzwalter was first seized with a fit of the gout in a very violent manner and with acute pain, which lasted till Friday night when it began to abate, but the ankle and foot continued very much swelled; during which time I gave Dr. Hollings £3 3s. 0d."

From that time onwards, apart from a few years in the early 1740s, she was subject to acute attacks which increased in frequency. From 1745 they were thrice at Tunbridge Wells and six times at Bath. The final spell at Bath lasted from January 9th to May 19th, 1751, and cost £962; the absence of entries for the next three weeks suggests that for once Fitzwalter found something even more serious than money to prey upon his mind.

Accompanied by his step-daughter and her husband and little daughter, Fitzwalter took his wife to Tunbridge Wells in July, but clearly it was only a palliative. There are no account book entries for August 6th–23rd (Lady Fitzwalter died on the 7th), and when they were resumed there are distinct signs of shakiness in the handwriting. Perhaps Lady Mary Wortley Montague's sneer was worth making: Fitzwalter *was* something of a bivalve (certainly he was a tight as a clam), but the old oyster loved his wife and missed her sorely.

It is worth recording that fairly frequent payments to doctors and apothecaries did not mean that illness dominated the household, except, perhaps, in the closing months of Lady Fitzwalter's life. Moreover, periods of illness were not necessarily times of unrelieved misery. No doubt some of these visits to Bath and Tunbridge Wells had their moments of gaiety and entertainment. Occasionally Fitzwalter lists his expenditure at the Spas in a certain amount of detail, but the separate 'Bath Book' which he kept has not survived; this would have been a valuable social document. There is, however, a record of a long holiday in 1736 which included some mild medical treatment:

> "Wednesday, June 30th. I set out from London with my wife and my Lord and Lady Ancram in order to go to Harrogate to drink the sulphur waters. We stayed a few days at York, and then went to Knaresborough and stayed there two months, and went from thence every morning to drink the sulphur and chalybeate waters, which is an hour's driving from the town with six horses. . . . The 8th September I set out southward . . . and arrived at Moulsham Hall, Friday, September 24th with eleven saddle horses, seven coach horses and also a hired coach and six from London. We were in all 22 or 23 in number?"

The roads in 1736 were far from good and coaches were virtually springless, but the North was still unscarred by industrial revolution; and it is pleasant to assume that the Yorkshire scenery and air did as much good to Lady Fitzwalter as the waters of Harrogate.

Medical—selective extracts

1725	July 30		£	s.	d.
	To Sir Hans Sloane for advice, who ordered me bitters and "Spaw" waters for one month		1	1	0

		£	s.	d.

1726   June 25
To Sir Hans Sloane for Lady Caroline. Her fever begins this day (*to*) abate, but abated much more the 29th. She began asses' milk the 28th   ...   .   — 1   1   0

Nov. 18
To Mr. Vilponteur for cleaning my teeth...   — 1   1   0

1727   Jan. 2
To Mr. Amiens, the surgeon, for attending Lady Caroline Darcy, and my son, Schomberg, during their inoculation, Lady Caroline's incision continuing to run above 8 weeks   ...   .   — 40   0   0

Jan. 22–24
To Sir Hans Sloane for my son, Schomberg, upon his rupture, teeth and fever...   — 3   3   0

To Mr. Amiens, surgeon, in the same account, for my son   ...   .   — 4   4   0

July 10
To Sir H. Sloane and Dr. Hollings on a consultation whether the Bath was proper for my Lady Holderness ...   .   — 2   2   0

Nov. 6
Spent in my journey to and from the Bath with a coach and six horses and 7 saddle horses. To the carriage by the waggon to and from the Bath. Spent at the Bath in ten weeks in expenses of all sorts, gaming excepted   ...   .   — 316   15   1

1728   Feb. 16
To Dr. Bowes, being the day my dear brother died, he having stayed and lain in the house 3 or 4 nights; gave him more than his daily fee ...   .   — 5   5   0

1729   Mar. 18
To Dr. Hollings for myself for ordering a purge, having a rheumatic pain in my arm   ...   .   — 1   1   0

		£	s.	d.

May 2
To Dr. Hollings on my wife's miscarrying this day of two children, being 3 months gone   1   1   0

June 28
To Mr. Garnier for attending my Lady Fitzwalter in taking two vomits   1   1   0

1731 Mar. 10
To Dr. Hollings, my wife being troubled with a stitch in her chest   1   1   0

May 15
To Mr. Amiens, the surgeon, £1 1s. 0d., for going to see a child my coachman drove over, but with doing him very little hurt; and to the child's mother, 10s. 6d. ...   1   11   6

May 28
To Dr. Hollings for my being out of order at my stomach, for which he gave me some rhubarb overnight and some hiera-pyera in the morning   1   1   0

July 21
To Mr. Garnier's man for dressing my Lady Fitzwalter's blister for a sort of stitch or rheumatic pains in her breast   1   1   0

1732 Aug. 12
To the dipper at the Islington well ...   0   10   6

1733 Oct. 6
N.B. This morning I took ten grains of ipecacuanha

1734 July 2–3
Gave Dr. Hollings for his advice on my having an indigestion   2   2   0

July 30
Pd. my Lady Fitzwalter a guinea, which she gave the surgeon for bleeding Lord Holderness in the neck on his having sore eyes   1   1   0

Oct. 4   £   s.   d.
Pd. Mr. Johnson, surgeon at Chelmsford,
curing a sore leg for Grutchfield, my
woodman   1   1   0

1736 Feb. 4
To Dr. Hollings for the Earl of Holderness
having a little sickness often at his
stomach and breaking out with large
heats and pimples upon his face   ...   1   1   0

To Mr. Hawkins, the surgeon, for bleeding
Lord Holderness 0 10   6

Apr. 29
To Dr. Hollings for my wife having a giddiness by drinking too much Islington water
the first day   ...   . (*not entered*)

June 3
I set out from London with my wife and
my Lord and Lady Ancram in order to
go to Harrogate to drink the sulphur
waters. We stayed a few days at York,
and then went to Knaresborough and
stayed there 2 months, and went from
thence every morning to drink the sulphur
and chalybeate waters, which is an hour's
driving from the town with six horses. At
York the Earl of Holderness came to us,
being gone into the north a few weeks
before we left Knaresborough. We went
to Hornby Castle, a seat of my Lord
Holderness's, where I kept house for 4
days, expen(ce) £14 0s. 0d. The 8th of
September I set out southward from
Knaresborough and stopped at another
house of my Lord Holderness's at Aston.
Stayed there nine days and spent in house-
keeping there, £22 0s. 0d. Then set out for
Newark, and so on to Peterborough to
make a visit to the Dean and lay at the
deanery one night. From there to Cam-

	£	s.	d.

June 3rd—*cont.*

bridge, so to Hockerill, and arrived at
Moulsham Hall, Friday, September 24th,
with eleven saddle horses, seven coachhorses and also a hired coach and six
from London. We were in all 22 or 23
in number, and often 6, 7 or 8 and twenty
upon the road. I spent on the expedition
from the last of June to September 24th,
1736 ... ... 530 0 0

Dec. 3

Gave Dr. Hollings upon my having a violent
cold and a little feverish, for which he
ordered me the wormwood draught at 2
several times 2 2 0

1737 Jan. 24

To Dr. Hollings on my having a numbness
and whiteness in one of my fingers ... 1 1 0

Feb. 3

To Dr. Hollings on my having a violent cold
and shooting pains all over me 1 1 0

Feb. 4

To Mr. Hawkins for taking away 11 ounces
of blood 1 1 0

June 9

To Dr. Hollings on my Lord Holderness
having a great flutter and palpitation of
heart 1 1 0

1738 July 13–14

To Wall, the apothecary's man, for trying to
cup my Lady Fitzwalter. N.B. the instrument very bad 0 10 0

To Dr. Coe for my Lady Fitzwalter having
a giddiness and a quick pulse 1 1 0

To—Mage of Chelmsford for bleeding my
Lady Fitzwalter in the jugular vein ... 1 1 0

	£	s.	d.

1739 Feb. 19

This morning at 5 o'clock my Lady Fitz-walter was first seized with a fit of the gout in a very violent manner and with very acute pain, which lasted till Friday night when it began to abate, but the ankle and foot continued very much swelled, during which time I gave Dr. Hollings 3 3 0

1740 Jan. 11

Pd. for the nurse-keeping and lodgings of Nutting, my 2nd coachman, during 9 days before he died of the small pox 2 2 0

May 28

Gave Mr. Hawkins, surgeon, for syringing both my ears, having been deaf on the left ear by a large quantity of wax for at least 3 weeks; by this, heard very well ... (*not entered*)

July 28

Pd. Lemage, the surgeon at Chelmsford, for attending Will Keys when he fell off a horse 3 3 0

Sept. 1

To Dr. Coe for attending my Lady Fitz-walter on her having a fit of the gout with a good deal of fever. N.B. She fell down and sprained both ankles, which brought on the gout. The pain lasted but 2 days 1 1 0

1742 Mar.–May

(*For interesting entries relating to Luke Crawforth, footman, see extracts in chapter on "My Family"*)

Aug. 26

Spent at Tunbridge in six weeks, viz: from July 6th to August 16th

Pd. for my lodgings at
£6 0s. 0d. per week   ...   36 0 0

Pd. for six coachhorses at
£3 6s. 4d. per week   ...   19 18 0

	£	s.	d.	£	s.	d.
Aug. 26th—*cont.*						
Pd. for nine horses at grass at 18s. per week ...	5	8	0			
Pd. for housekeeping the 1st week	21	6	0			
Pd. for the housekeeping the 2nd week	20	12	0			
Pd. for the housekeeping the 3rd week	19	0	3			
Pd. for the 4th week ...	18	14	0			
Pd. for the 5th week ...	16	17	6			
Pd. for the 6th week ...	13	2	6			
Gave the dipper for my Lady Fitzwalter and myself	2	2	0			
Gave the maidservants of the house I hired, Mrs. White's	3	3	0			
Gave to the servants of the two Great Rooms ...	1	1	0			
All expenses included, I spent not less than				200	0	0

1746 Jan. 21

Gave Mr. Hawkins, the surgeon, for Longmore my *valet de chambre* who had a bone stuck in his throat 10 10 0

1747 Nov. 10

Gave to the hospital at Bath 10 10 0

1748 Mar. 6

Gave Dr. Beaumont for attending me 5 or 6 times in order to remove a little complaint in one of my eyes—veritable charlatan 4 4 0

Mar. 25

Gave Mr. Hawkins for curing my toe of a humour that had fallen into it 5 5 0

		£	s.	d.

Dec. 10

Pd. —, nurse-keeper, for nursing Thos. Daw,
my house porter and a housemaid, both
in the small-pox last summer 10 3 0

1751 Jan. 9

Set out with my Lady Fitzwalter, and Dr.
Pringle with us, for the Bath

May 19

Arrived at London from Bath with my Lady
Fitzwalter and my Lady Louisa.
Spent on the road in going and coming
back, and by the carriage of goods, and
during our stay in Bath, with doctors'
fees there for my Lady Fitzwalter,
£912 0s. 0d., besides fifty pound I gave
to Pringle for only going down with us
and staying but 2 days, £50 0s. 0d. ... 962 0 0

CHAPTER SEVEN

INCOME AND INVESTMENT POLICY

Any examination of Fitzwalter's finances is bound to be a reminder of his alleged meanness. Before his account books became publicly available some thirty-odd years ago, the only so-called evidence for this meanness was a letter of May 10th, 1728, from Dean Swift to Lord Carteret. Swift's intention was to raise a monument in St. Patrick's to the great Schomberg, Lady Fitzwalter's grandfather. He had written to the Fitzwalters for a contribution and had received no reply. In this letter to Carteret he wrote that Fitzwalter "is a covetous fellow" and that Sir Conyers Darcy, brother of Lord Holderness, Lady Fitzwalter's first husband, had "averred that Mildmay (*i.e. Fitzwalter*) was so avaricious a wretch that he would let his own father be buried without a coffin to save charges". There is no evidence whatsoever to show that Fitzwalter was covetous; and although Darcy (who had fought a lawsuit with Fitzwalter and lost) might well have said those words, he did not say that Fitzwalter *had* let his father be buried coffinless. Indeed, at the time of his father's death Fitzwalter was barely seven years old!

But how mean is mean? Swift's barbs were cruelly pointed and they stuck; but account books are *reliable* evidence, often better than any letters or diaries. Again and again there are entries (many of them reproduced in this book) which show that Fitzwalter was extremely tight over money; he watched every ha'penny and saw to it that he always obtained the utmost value for any expenditure. But this does not seem to have been accompanied by any real meanness of spirit, and there are occasions, quoted in this book, when he could be almost generous. There are times, too, when he spent freely and willingly. There are no absolutes by which to judge, but even if he cannot be acquitted of meanness, he was certainly not guilty of avarice and covetousness.

158

When he married in 1724 and for another four years until his brother died, Fitzwalter was probably a landless man apart from owning oyster-layings in the River Crouch. Since his coming of age in 1693, he had had a private income of £1,000 a year secured on the family's Burnham estates, and he had another £1,000 in salary as a Commissioner of Excise. He owned South Sea stock worth £4,150; but he was also paying 5% interest on a bond of £4,000 to Sir John Newton and on his wife's bond of £2,000 to Lady Darlington. On the day of his wedding he had £387 in cash.

His marriage and his succession to his brother's title and estate gave him the opportunity to become rich. His income was considerably increased—he had more money available for investment and he could watch his capital and income grow. It is difficult to follow this growth step by step as some of the evidence has not survived, but it is possible to make spot checks on both income and capital. The year 1739 is a good one for a check on income as the Chelmsford and Moulsham rent book exists for that year—

		£
(1)	Post Office annuity ...	2,000
(2)	Household salary ...	1,200
(3)	Rent charge on the Earl of Holderness's estate ...	1,500
(4)	Rents from France ...	300
(5)	Exchequer Office annuities ...	100
(6)	Bank of England stock dividends ...	385
(7)	East India Company stock dividends ...	70
(8)	Burnham oyster-laying rents ...	160
(9)	Profits on lands in hand, say ...	100
(10)	Chelmsford and Moulsham rents ...	1,108
(11)	Chelmsford and Moulsham manorial dues	110
(12)	Burnham rents, say ...	950
(13)	Burnham manorial dues, say ...	90
		8,073

Most of these items call for some comment—

(1) *Post Office Annuity*, £2,000. This came through his wife and continued after her death in 1751. Originally it had been £4,000 a year granted to Meinhardt, Duke of Schomberg, by the nation in recognition of his own and his father's services. Schomberg left it jointly to his two daughters, Frederica, Fitz-

walter's wife, and Mary, wife of Count Dagenfeldt, the Prussian Minister to the Court of St. James. However, Lady Mary's share was bought by her brother-in-law, the 3rd Earl of Holderness, who had incumbered it with a debt of £36,000. In 1728, on the instructions of Sir Conyers Darcy, the brother of Lord Holderness and executor of his estates, Fitzwalter sold £1,000 a year of this £2,000 to Sir Michael Newton for £22,500, and the other £1,000 to Mr. Thomas Walker for an unspecified sum. Anyway, the net result was that Lady Fitzwalter's original £2,000 a year remained intact, and from the sale of the other half, Fitzwalter was able to pay off the debt and have a fair amount left over; at any rate, after the sale of the first £1,000 per annum he writes, "There rests in my hands and for my benefit, £5,335 0s. 5d."

(2) *Household Salary*, £1,200. This Treasureship of the King's Household he held from 1737 to 1755.

(3) *Rent charge on the Earl of Holderness's estate*, £1,500. This he drew throughout his wife's life time, paying her £500 as pin-money!

(4) *Rents from France*, £300, *but variable*. This, again, seems to have been part of his wife's legacy from Schomberg.

The remaining items were regarded by Fitzwalter as "my own money". The Chelmsford and Moulsham rents and dues are accurate; those from Burnham may be slightly underestimated but should be compared with the actual figures given in a rent list of *c.* 1756 (Hampshire Record Office, 15M 50/110). The figure given for profit from lands in hand is little more than a guess—it could be much higher, but not likely to be more than £250. One or two items should be added to this 1739 list. There was a small income, probably averaging £17–18 from investments in Holland, and there was an annual £5 1s. 6d. "cushion money", a perquisite of the office of Treasurer of the Household. In his left-hand-page entries, Fitzwalter recorded most, but not all, of his income for 1739. These entries are fully recorded in this chapter. It should be added that income from most sources was liable to Land Tax, which varied from 1s. to 4s. in the pound; in 1739 it was 2s. in the pound.

The 1739 list may be regarded as the standard pattern of Fitzwalter's income to 1751. The only difference is that the total increased, and the increase was almost wholly due to larger dividends from increased investments.

Fitzwalter had some significant *temporary* sources of income, both before and after 1739. Earlier, while his stepchildren were young, he was paid £400 a year out of the Holderness estates for the maintenance of Lord Holderness and £300 for Lady Caroline. For a short period, from September 1729 to August 1732, there were six mysterious payments, the first of £1,000, the others of £500. These are marked in his account book as being from "W" usually a W with a rounded base and a horizontal line across the top of the middle minim. Almost certainly, these represent payments from Walpole. In 1733, there is one more payment of £1,000, but this entered as received from "X". Later, there are several more entries which are more explicit—

1737 Feb. 15	£	s.	d.

"Rec'd from S(*i*)r Rob(*er*)t Walpole one
yearly allowance from the King over
and above the £1,000 a year as first
Lord Com(*missione*)r of the Board of
Trade, w(*hi*)ch is in full of that £500
p(er) ann(*um*) to Nov(embe)r 21st last
past   500   0   0"

In the 1740s, some of Fitzwalter's income came from money lent to his stepson, but he had to sell stock to provide some of the money and he charged Holderness only 4%, well below the rate he would have received from Bank dividends.

*   *   *   *   *

His investment policy was probably the simplest and best ever devised for non-inflationary times—he lived well within his income, and he invested his savings in gilt-edged securities, mainly Bank of England stock. It is not easy to follow his transactions: the only evidence are scrappy and somewhat illegible notes on the inside covers or early pages of his account books. Moreover, the figures do not represent the full extent of his growing prosperity, for throughout the period 1728–*c*.1749 he was paying out large sums for the rebuilding and embellishment of Moulsham Hall. However, it seems that in January 1728, only 3½ years after his marriage, he sold his remaining South Sea stock, and in January and February of that year he bought £3,000 Bank of England stock. This seems to be the extent of his "savings", but as he had earlier sold £1,500 South Sea stock to help redeem Lady Fitzwalter's bond of £2,000 to the executors of Lady Darlington, and another £500 to help pay for lottery tickets which he then sold to his friends, he was not doing too badly! Between that date and July 1739, he bought more parcels of Bank stock, £6,000 in all, costing him £8,124 7s. 6d.

Early in 1734, he seems to have sold all his existing Bank stock. Anyhow, on May 17th, 1734, he paid into the Bank of England £10,426 8s. in bank notes. Then he began reinvesting in Bank stock and some East India company stock using this money, the last £500 of which he drew in December 1736, and, presumably, his "savings" as from 1734. He gives details of his buying and selling between November 6th, 1735, and October 16th, 1741, and notes that on October 17th, 1741, "I have at this time Ten Thousand pounds Capital stock in the Bank of England". The rate on the previous days was 139¾; thus, his holding was then worth £13,975.

In his next town account book (D/DM A7) he records later transactions, and concludes, "Janry 17th, 1752, I have this day Capital Bank stock of £17,000." This, on the previous day's rate of 143, was then worth £24,310. In addition, he states that he holds bank annuities of £3,000.

His Will (D/DM T96/22) reflected the result of long years of thrift—perhaps, parsimony. His estates went to his cousin, Sir William Mildmay. He left £2,000 to his faithful steward, Edward Johnson, and reasonable sums to other servants. A trust fund of £6,000 was set up for his step-daughter, Lady Ancram, and to her daughter, the little Lady Louisa Kerr, the consolation of his last years as an old widower (*see* chapter on "My Family") he left the considerable sum of £18,000. Louisa lived to be over 90, and it would be pleasant if some curious historian, with time to spare, would endeavour to find out if that old lady left any memoirs of years long ago and of an old man who was not as flinty-hearted as Swift would have posterity believe.

References
    Dean Swift's letter, mentioned in the first paragraph, is printed by *The Complete Peerage* (under Fitzwalter).

Income and Investment Policy
Fitzwalter's record of his income for the year, 1739 *(D/DM A6)*
N.B. He has not included his income from some sources.
Original spelling retained.

	£	s.	d.
Jan(ua)ry 13th Recd. from the Bank of England my Divi- dend for half a year, due Michmas, 1738	192	10	0
Jan(ua)ry 18th Recd. at my Lord Macclesfield's office at the Exch(e)q(ue)r three Quarters' Interest due on my 2 annuity orders at Michmas, 1738	75	0	0
Jan(ua)ry 15th Recd. Christmas divid(en)d at the India House due on £2,000 stock	70	0	0
Feb(rua)ry 8th Recd. from the Post-Office the Quarter's annuity due at Christmas last past, in mony. £447 10s. 0d., by Fees allow'd by me, £2 10s. 0d., allow'd also, £50 for the Q(uarte)r's Land Tax	500	0	0
Feb(rua)ry 10th Recd. by the hands of Mr. John Mason the Quarter's rent due at Christmas last from James Buxton and Rob(er)t Hurst, oyster- Dredgers and the present tenants to the River of Burnham, al(ia)s Walfleet, and in full	40	0	0
Feb(rua)ry 20th Recd. by the hands of Mr. Skinner the Quarter's salary due to me at Michmas, 1738, as Treas(ure)r of his Majesty's House, in mony, £244 16s. 6d., by Land Tax and by other deductions, £55 3s. 6d.	300	0	0
Feb(rua)ry 28th Recd. by the hands of Mr. Mathew Lamb the half year's rent-Charge on the Earl of Holdernesse's Estate, due at Martinmas			

	£	s.	d.

last to the Countess Fitz-Walter, deduct-
ing for the Land-Tax at 2s. *p(er)* pound,
£23, and in mony, £727 0s. 0d., in all, in
full   750   0   0

April 18th
Rec(*eive*)d the half year's Divid(*en*)d due at
Lady-day last past on £7,000 Cap(*i*)t(*a*)ll-
stock in the Bank of England 192 10   0

May 4th
Rec(*eive*)d from Monsr. de Villemonote a
bill drawn upon Mr. (*blank*) Nesbit in
Coleman-street for 3450 Livres Tournois,
being the half year's rent due on the Hôtel
de Ville de Paris the 1st of Jan(*ua*)ry,
1739, N.B., in English mony   149   2   9

May 7th
Rec(*eive*)d by the hands of Mr. Skinner the
Quarter's salary due to me at Christmas
last out of the Cofferer's-office, in Nett
mony, £289 16s. 6d., allow'd to Civil-List
duty, £7 10s. 0d., to Cofferer's-office,
£1 12s. 6d., Debenture Fee, £1 1s. 0d., in
all   300   0   0

May 11th
Rec(*eive*)d from the Post-Office the Q(*uarte*)r's annuity due at Lady-day, 1739, in
mony, £447 10s., by Fees allow'd by me,
£2 10s. 0d., allow'd also for the Q(*uar-
te*)r's L(*an*)d Tax, £50   500   0   0

Sept(*embe*)r 25th
Rec(*eive*)d by the hands of Mr. Skinner the
Quarter's salary due to me at Lady-day
as Treasurer of his Majesty's Household,
in mony, £244 16s. 6d., by L(*an*)d Tax at
2s. *p(er)* p(*ai*)d and by other deductions
£55 3s. 6d.   300   0   0

	£	s.	d.

Sep(tembe)r 27th
Rec(*eive*)d from the Post-Office the Q(*uar-te*)r's annuity due to me at Midsummer, 1739, in mony, £447 10s. 0d., by fees allow'd by me, £2 10s. 0d., and by the Q(*uarte*)r's Land Tax, £50, en tout ...   500   0   0

October 15th
Rec(*eive*)d at my Lord Macclesfeild's-office at the Excheq(*ue*)r three Q(*uarte*)rs' of a year's Interest due on my Two annuity orders at Mich(*ael*)mas, 1739   75   0   0

October 26th
Rec(*eive*)d of the Earl of Ancram, £5 5s. 0d., w(*hi*)ch my steward in Essex paid at (*my*) Lord's desire to his serv(*an*)t at Chelmsford   5   5   0

Nov(embe)r 1st
Rec(*eive*)d from the Board of Green-Cloth, 4 Warr(*an*)ts for Does, w(*i*)th the usual Fees for the Keepers-mony   1   6   8

Nov(embe)r 14th
Rec(*eive*)d by the hands of Mr. Skinner the Quarter's salary due to me as Treas(*ure*)r of his Majesty's Household at Midsummer, 1739, in Nett mony, £289, Civil List Fee, £7 10s. 0d., Cofferer's-office, £1 12s. 6d., Debenture Fee, £1 1s. 0d. ...   300   0   0

Nov(embe)r 19th
Rec(*eive*)d of Mr. Beal for Carpet and Cushion-mony   5   1   6

Nov(embe)r 21st
Rec(*eive*)d at the Bank, the Mich(*ael*)mas Divid(*en*)d, 1739, in £7000 Cap(*i*)t(*a*)ll Bk.-stock   500   0   0

Nov(embe)r 29th
Rec(*eive*)d from the Post-Office the Quarter's annuity due at Mich(*ael*)mas last, L(*an*)d Tax allow'd, £50   500   0   0

	£	s.	d.

Dec(embe)r 13th
Rec(*eive*)d from Monsr. De Villemenote a bill drawn by Monsr. Alexander upon Bart. Burton for the value of 3450 Livres Tournois, being the Rents due on the Hôtel de Ville de six premiere Mois de l'annee, 1739, in English mony 150 6 9

Dec(embe)r 15th

Rec(*eive*)d of Mr. Matt. Lamb the Half-year's rent-charge due from the Estates of the Earl of Holdernesse to the Countesse Fitz-Walter at Martinmas, 1739, in mony, £727, by L(*an*)d Tax at 2s. p(*er*) pound, £23 0s. 0d. 750 0 0

Income and Investment Policy   selective extracts
Original spelling retained

1724   July 30
     Sold Ten Lottery Tickets at £1 9s. p(*re*)mium   114 5 0

1726   May 26
     Rec(*eive*)d from the Post-Office one Q(*uarte*)rs annuity on £3000 p(*er*) ann(*um*), due Lady day last past, £1000 p(*er*) ann(*um*) being sold to Mr. Tho(*ma*)s Walker before Lady day last, £75 being allow'd for Taxes. Receiv'd in Net mony 675 0 0

     Sept. 9
     Sold £1500 Capitall South sea stock at $104\frac{1}{2}$ p(*er*) c(*en*)t. in order to pay off my Lady Holdernesse's Bond of £2000 due to the Executors of my Lady Darlington   ...   1567 10 0

1727   Nov. 8
     At Popes Rec(*eive*)d for Drover's Cattel Lying in my fields 3 18 0

     For Pidgeons sold 10 0

     For 8 Dozen of Rabbits sold at 9s. p(*er*) Dozen, Deducting for Carrying up, 13s., am(*oun*)ts to 2 19 0

	£	s.	d.

1728 June 28

The remains of the Purchase mony of £1000
p(er) ann(um) annuity in the Post-Office
sold to Michael Newton for £22,500, after
all incumberances were discharg(e)d, and
£250 pd. to Mr. Lamb, to pay the fine
w(*hi*)ch was to be levied in order to con-
vey the sd. £1000 annuity. There Rests in
my hands and for my benefit, £5335 0s. 5d. **5335 0 0**

June 29

Rec(*eive*)d from the Excise-Office the Quarters Salary due Midsum(*m*)er last past, my
place not being filled up till this 24th of
June, the salary became due to me tho' I
never attended the Board since the death
of my Brother Fitzwalter, Land-Tax for
this Q(*uarte*)r already paid, £28 2s. 6d.,
also Sixpenny Poundage allow'd, £6
5s. 0d., rec(*eive*)d in Net Mony **215 12 6**

Aug. 13

Rec(*eive*)d from Denzel Onslow, post-office,
the Quarter's annuity due June 24th last
past, Land-Tax at 3 shill. in the pound
being allow'd, seventy five pound, and in
ready mony **425 0 0**

N.B. One Thousand pounds a year of the
sd. annuity being sold to Mr. Thos.
Walker and one other Thousand pounds
a (*year*) of it being sold to S(*i*)r Michael
Newton very lately, so that £2000 *p(er)
ann(um)* only remains, w(*hi*)ch £2000
p(er) ann(um) was my wife's part of the
£4000 *p(er)* ann(um) left by Duke Schonburg to his 2 Daughters, and the other
£200(0) *p(er) ann(um)* was purchas'd of
Lady Mary Degenfeldt by my Lord Holdernesse, who also incumber'd it w(*i*)th a
debt of £36,000, for w(*hi*)ch reason that
£2000 *p(er) ann(um)* so encumber'd was
was sold by me and my wife and the

	£	s.	d.

whole debt paid off, part of w(hi)ch was
£10,000 for Lady Caroline's fortune, by
order of S(i)r Conyers Darcy as executor
to the Earl of Holdernesse his Brother
deceas'd.

Dec. 4

Sold six Bullocks to my Butcher Mr. Dole-
man in St. James's market, fed at Moul-
shaum Hall, for 42 0 0

1729 May 31

Rec(eive)d from Count Degenfeld by the
hands of Mr. Vanderesch the sum of £25
4s. 7d. w(hi)ch w(i)th Ten Guineas I
allow'd being Godfather to one of his
children makes £35 14s. 7d., and is for
two years interest for the half of 12,600
florins in a Fund in Holland belonging to
my wife and the other half to Lady Mary 35 14 7

Sept. 14

Recd. from W(alpole) 1000 0 0

1730 Jan. 7

Rec(eive)d from Mr. James Camper sole
Tenant of the River of Burnham one
Quarters Rent for the sd. River due at
Christmas last past, but gave him only a
rec(eip)t for so much on acco(un)t ... 40 0 0

1731 Dec. 20

Rec(eive)d also at the same time of Mr.
Lamb on the Acco(un)t of my *Lady* Caroline Darcy's maintenance for half a year
ending Nov(embe)r 26th last past ... 150 0 0

1733 May 10

Rec(eive)d from X due at Christmas last the
sum of 1000 0 0

1734 Jan. 12

Rec(eive)d (Mr. Lamb) half a year's maintenance for my Lady Caroline Darcy, due
Nov(embe)r 20th last past 150 0 0

	£	s.	d.

May 13

Rec(*eive*)d by the hands of Mr. Lamb the
Q(*uarte*)r's allowance for the maintenance
of the Earl of Holdernesse, due the 20th
of April, 1734   ...   .   100 0 0

May 16

Rec(*eive*)d of Mr. Cavarly, Confectioner, for
a Load of Charcoal sent last year out of
the Country 4 10 0

1736 May 20

There are in the Hôtel de Ville de Paris
28,600 Livres Tournois Capitall. The
yearly rents 2½ p(*er*) c(*en*)t, amount to
7150 Livres. The half yearly to 3575. The
said rents are at present and for some time
have been rec(*eive*)d by Monsr. de
Villemenot at 200 Livres Tournois yearly
for his trouble.

1737 Feb. 15

Rec(*eive*)d from S(*i*)r Rob(*er*)t Walpole one
year allowance from the King over and
above the £1000 a year as first Lord Com-
(*missione*)r of the Board of Trade, w(*hi*)ch
is in full for that £500 p(*er*) ann(*um*) to
Nov(*embe*)r 21st last past 500 0 0

1743 Apr. 29

I lent the Earl of Holdernesse the sum of
Two Thousand pounds at 3½ p(*er*) cent
Interest, on his House at Whitehall   ... 2000 0 0

1744 July 7th

The Earl of Holdernesse discharg'd the said
mortgage, repd. me the £2000 I had lent
him, w(*i*)th the Interest in full to this day,
being £95

1745 Sept.

I sold £2000 Capital Bank Stock in order to
make up the sum of Four Thousand
pound to pay the debts the Earl of Holderness had contracted at Venice, w(*hi*)ch
sum of Four Thousand pounds I lent him
and was by my order Pd. into the hands

	£	s.	d.

of Mr. Mat. Lamb his agent and for use, October 14th or 15th, 1745, and Pd. by Messrs. Snow and Deane, my Bankers.

1747   Mar. 2

Rec(*eive*)d by the hands of a serv(*an*)t of the Duke of Devonshire (Lord Steward) the Cushion-mony annually due to me as Treas(ure)r of his Majesty's Household...   5   1   6

1748   Dec. 22

Lent to the Earl of Holdernesse the sum of Two Thousand pound at the Interest of Four *p*(*er*) *Cent.* for w(*hi*)ch all his service of Wrought Plate is made over to me and is now lying in the hands of Messrs. Snow and Deane as my security.

N.B. I have allow'd my Lord Holdernesse to make use of this Plate and to carry it w(*i*)th him into Holland, for w(*hi*)ch he has by way of security given me his Bond.

Mar. 10

Lent the Earl of Holdernesse four Thousand pound more, at an Interest of Four *p*(*er*) *Cent*, for the security of w(*hi*)ch I have my Lord's Bond and an assignm(*en*)t of a Contract for Timber for £1780 to be paid in three years, and also a promise of another Timber Contract of about £1200, w(*hi*)ch is to be assigned over to me

1750   Dec. 7

Rec(*eive*)d for 22 sheep sold by me here, at London   22   0   0

Income and Investment Policy—Fitzwalter's notes on investments from one of his account books (D/DM A6)
Original spelling retained

(On inside cover of book)   £

I have in Capital Bank Stock, June 2(*n*)d, 1733   7,800

Aug(*u*)st 30th, 1733, Bought £200 Cap(*i*)t(*a*)ll B(*an*)k stock at 146   200

8,000

Feb(*rua*)ry 8th, 1733, sold and Transferr(*e*)d to S(*i*)r W(*illia*)m
Heathcote, 2,000 Cap(*i*)t(*a*)ll B(*an*)k Stock at 130½ *p(er) C(en)t*
mony recd. £2610.

May 17th, 1734, I paid into the Bank of England in Bank notes,
£10,426 8s. 0d., for w(*hi*)ch I have a Bank book by w(*hi*)ch
they own themselves Debt(*o*)rs to me for that sum

£10,426 8 0

N.B. Mr. John Mitford, Broker, was by when I paid it in and
took this book.

N.B. The India and Bank stock, mention'd on the other side
to be bought, was paid for out of the mony mentione'd as
above lying in the Bank, and is set off by my Bank-book.

N.B. I have drawn out of the Bank at times as on the first leaf is
mentioned in this book for the Purchase of stocks every part
of the sum of £10,426 8s. 0d. above mention'd, except the sum
of £500, w(*hi*)ch is still lying there this 29th day of June, 1736

£500 0 0

N.B. Dec(*embe*)r 1736, I have now drawn out of the Bank the £500
above mention'd, and have now no mony lying there but what
is actually invested in their Capit(*a*)ll stock.

(On facing first page of book) £ *s.* *d.*

Nov(*embe*)r 6th, 1735, Bought Three Thousand
    pounds Cap(*i*)t(*a*)ll India-stock at 159¾ w(*hi*)ch
    cost me 4,792 10 0
    N.B. Feb(*rua*)ry 28th, 1737, sold £1000 of this
    stock at 177.

Jan(*ua*)ry 21st, 1735, Bought Two Thousand pounds
    Capitall Bank-stock at £149 and ¾ *p(er) C(en)t*,
    w(*hi*)ch cost 2,993 15 0

Feb(*rua*)ry 4th, 1735, Bought this day one Thousand
    pounds Capital Bank-stock at 148 *p(er) C(en)t*,
    w(*hi*)ch cost 1,480 0 0

June 28th, 1736, Bought and paid for this day to
    Mathew Lesterenon, a Dutch-man, £1000
    Cap(*i*)t(*a*)ll Bank-stock at £149 *p(er) C(en)t* ...   1,490 0 0

Dec(embe)r 17th, 1736, Bought and paid for £500
    Cap(*i*)t(*a*)ll Bank-Stock at 149 *p(er) Cent* of
    Two Execut(*o*)rs Henry & Mary Sladen, Cost   749 0 0

11,505 0 0
(*sic*)

Sept. 7th, 1737 Bought and paid for £500 Cap(i)t(a)l Bank-stock at 145½ p(er) C(en)t w(hi)ch cost ... £ s. d. 722 15 0

Feb(rua)ry 23rd, 1737. Bought and Paid for £1000 Cap(i)t(a)ll Bank-stock of Henry Lovibond at 141 p(er) C(en)t 1,410 0 0

13,637 5 0

(sic)

Feb(rua)ry 28th, 1737. Sold one Thousand pound of Capit(a)ll India-stock at 170 p(er) C(en)t, w(hi)ch produc'd £1770, and Bought this day one Thousand pounds Cap(i)t(a)ll Bank-stock at 142 p(er) C(en)t, for w(hi)ch I paid 1,420 0 0

N.B. Balance resting in my hands between selling and buying, £350.

May 18th, 1738, sold this day £2000 Capital India-stock at 168½ p(er) C(en)t, w(hi)ch amounted to 3,370 0 0

Dec(embe)r 5th, 1740, Bought £2000 Capital Bank-stock at 139½ w(hi)ch cost 2,792 10 0

N.B. This £2000 Bank-stock was bought for me by Mr. Snow, Senior, the Banker, and enter'd in the Books of the Bank in my name by virtue of a Letter of Attorny w(hi)ch I gave him for that purpose, and pd. the sd. Mr. Thos. Snow the purchase-mony of sd. stock bo(ugh)t on my acco(un)t, Dec(embe)r, 1740, being as above, £2792 10s. 0d.

Oct(ober) 16th, 1741 Pd. for £100 Capital Bank-Stock Transferr'd to my name by letter of Attorny to Mr. (*blank*) Deane, b(ough)t at 139¾, Cost 1,398 15 0

CHAPTER EIGHT

ENTERTAINMENT AND THE ARTS

The evidence suggests that Fitzwalter was not a man who frequently needed to be entertained. When he was in the country, at Moulsham Hall, he was precluded from the normal field sports by his paralysed arm, and, while he occasionally entertained his friends and kinsmen and was himself entertained, there are no account book entries to indicate that he was caught up in any kind of social whirl. He seemed quite content to stay put with his family, to watch his house being built and to supervise and contribute to its adornment—and to play cards. Occasionally there would be a little change—an excursion to see Blenheim and Oxford (*see extacts under Personal Transport*) or a visit to his estates in the Dengie Hundred, with a trip up the river Crouch.

In Town, the public offices he held and his wife's social eminence secured him a place in Court and government circles, and thus an adequate amount of entertainment—at no additional cost to himself! Indeed, the antics of the Royal family alone should have ensured this, though he may not have had Lord Hervey's eye for black comedy. Otherwise, he enjoyed himself quietly and frugally. Twice he gave a ball at Schomberg House, and several times he entertained Sir Robert Walpole and other dignitaries to dinner. He maintained boxes at Drury Lane and the Haymarket until 1742, and probably at Covent Garden. He attended at least one of Count Heidegger's ridottos. He bought lottery tickets and was not above a little profitable dealing in them. Over the space of 20 years he bought 3 new chess-boards and 5 sets of chessmen.

*　　　*　　　*　　　*　　　*

A man who spent £43 a year on tea and coffee, £90 on claret, £360 on personal transport and only £8 on books could scarcely be called a bookworm. Occasionally, no doubt, he was conned or shamed by his friends and acquaintances into subscribing to an author's forthcoming book—it is difficult, for example, to imagine him actually reading Stephen Duck's poetry; otherwise, his tastes could be called catholic rather than intensive. Famous names occur. He subscribed to Pope's Homer's *Odyssey,* Voltaire's *Henriade* and Leoni's two great works. He bought Camden's *Britannia,* Richelieu's *Memoirs,* D'Ewes' *Journal,* Sir William Temple's works, Bishop Burnet's *History,* Steele's *Plays,* Campbell's *Vitruvius,* Charles Jervas's translation of *Don Quixote* and 8 volumes of *The Spectator.* He was interested in classical history and in contemporary, or near contemporary, memoirs and topographical works in English and French. He bought some practical books: James Postlethwayt's *History of the Public Revenues,* Ephraim Chambers's *Dictionary,* a builder's dictionary, one of Jethro Tull's books and two of Batty Langley's, a custom-house book of wine tables and Arthur Collins's *Precedent of Claims on Baronies.*

*   *   *   *   *

Posterity is entitled to look kindly upon Fitzwalter for his patronage of de Lamerie (see chapter on *Running a Household*); probably he would not have regarded it in this way, but merely as buying good table equipment from a good craftsman. In no other way could he be regarded as a liberal patron of the arts. Between 1726 and 1747 he spent nearly £300 on pictures and framing, mostly to decorate his new Moulsham Hall. He paid 30 guineas to "Mr. Cox, the auctioneer, for a picture bought at Sir Godfrey Kneller's sale of the Marshal, Duke Schomberg on horseback, my wife's grandfather." In 1742 "at Mrs. Howe's auction, who was daughter to Prince Rupert", he bought a large picture of the Palatine family painted by Honthorst; Prince Rupert's elder brother, Charles Louis, Elector Palatine, was Lady Fitzwalter's other (maternal) grandfather. After the picture had been cleaned and reframed, it was taken down to Moulsham Hall. He commissioned Enoch Seeman to paint "my picture at length, now at Moulsham Hall in Essex, and in robes" for 20 guineas. He commissioned Andrea Soldi to paint portraits of Lord Holderness, his stepson, and Lord Ancram, his stepdaughter's husband. He bought a Rembrandt (or so he thought) for 5 guineas in 1741. In 1742 he paid 10 guineas to "Mr. John Wootton for retouching, mending and improving a landscape, originally of his own painting. N.B. it cost me at an auction, £16 5s. 6d., besides what I gave to Mr. Wootton. There is in this

picture a white horse a-feeding. I have sent it down this day to
Moulsham Hall." At the Smyrna Coffee House he paid 3 guineas
"for a picture of a horse of the Duke of Devonshire's, called
Childers, with a rubbing-groom in blue, holding the horse by the
bridle, and riding-groom upon a grey cropped horse holding up
one foot". He paid 10 guineas "for a fowl piece, with a peacock
in it at large" by Stranovius; he bought flower prints from Robert
Hunton and prints of the defeat of the Armada by John Pine.

Entertainment—selective extracts

		£	s.	d.
1726	Sept. 14			
	From 40 lottery tickets sold at £9 12s. 6d.	375	0	0
1729	Feb. 4			
	Subscribed to Count Heidegger for an opera next winter, 15 guineas, of which pd. down £5 5s.	5	5	0
	Feb. 12			
	To a benefit ticket to my Lady Teynham for a new play	1	1	0
1730	Jan. 23			
	Pd. Mr. Upton for 3 tickets for *Sophonisba*	3	3	0
1732	May 24			
	Pd. for a newspaper for one year called *Daily Advertiser*	1	4	0
1733	Mar. 15			
	To Madame D'Acunha for a raffle ...	1	1	0
	Apr. 26			
	For a ticket to go to the *Ridotto*	1	6	0
1734	Jan. 9			
	Lost at Quadrille	8	0	0
	Jan. 10			
	Lost at 'Whisk'	3	3	0
	Jan. 11			
	Gave to the boxkeeper in the Haymarket Playhouse		10	6
	Jan. 15			
	To the expenses of plays and operas for my Lady Holderness	2	2	0

		£	s.	d.

Apr. 5
To Joseph Haynes by order of the directors of the opera in Lincoln Inn Fields for this year, being in the whole, 20 guineas, having pd. 15 before and 5 guineas now ... 5 5 0

1735 Jan. 3
Gave half a guinea to the box keepers at Drury Lane 10 6

Gave to the box keepers at Covent Garden playhouse 10 6

Feb. 25
To operas, plays and other petty expenses 5 5 0

June 3
Advanced to my Lady Fitzwalter after a bad run at cards 10 10 0

1736 Nov. 28
Gave Wilkins's son for bringing me a ticket for the Westminster School acting-plays 1 1 0

1737 Jan. 8
To Mr. Powell, harper, for playing one evening 1 0 0

July 6
Went to Burnham Hall with my Lady Fitz-walter, the Earl of Holderness, the Earl and Countess of Ancram, dined and lay there and the 7th returned again after dinner hither. Gave the ringers, £1 1s. Went on board Saywell's sloop and sailed up the river in the afternoon on the 6th. Gave the sailors, £2 2s. Pd. the butcher's bill, £1 0s. 6d. Pd. Mr. Clarke, the farmer at the Hall, his bill, £3 0s. 9d. Gave the maid 10s. In all, having sixteen horses and being 17 people in number 7 14 3

1738 July 29
Pd. Longmore, my butler, his bill in full for 35 packs of cards and 2 journeys to London 3 6 8

		£	s.	d.
1740	Jan. 17			
	Gave to the music that played at a ball I gave here this day	6	6	0
1741	Oct. 26			
	Pd. the Earl of Holderness my subscription for the winter's opera and received a silver ticket	21	0	0
	Nov. 23			
	Pd. for two tickets in the Bridges lottery begin to be drawn today	12	0	0
1743	Feb. 26			
	To my Lady Ancram towards making a stock-purse for her to play at cards ...	10	10	0
1749	Apr. 27			
	Pd. — Buckland for a set of chess-men, half ivory, the knights with nags' heads and necks, the other half made of cocoa ...	1	5	0

Books—transcript of all relevant entries
Original spelling retained

		£	s.	d.
1724	Apr. 16			
	To Lady Holderness in full of a subscription to Mr. Pope for Homer's Odyssey ...	2	2	0
	May 31			
	Mr. Degrave, Bookseller, for a Q(*uar*)to set of State Tryals	2	2	0
1726	May 12			
	To Mr. Leoni in part of a subscription for his 3 volumes of Architecture, one being then deliver'd	3	3	0
	Sept. 20			
	Laid out in books 14s. 6d., lost at Cards, £2, and given away, £1, in all	3	14	6
	Oct. 16			
	To Dr. Boorhaave's book of Chemistry ...		18	0
1727	May 12			
	To Monsr. Volterre for a subscript(*io*)n ...	2	2	0

		£	s.	d.

June 20
To Jacob Tonson for Bayle's Dictionary,
2(n)d Edit.   2   5   0

Nov. 16
To Monsr. De Noyee for 4 vol. of Timur
Bec & 6 vol. of Brantome's Hommes
Illustres   1   0   0

1728   Mar. 26
To Mr. Voltaire in full of the subscription
to his book, call'd the Henriade   2   2   0

To Signior Leoni, the 2(n)d paym(en)t of a
subscription to 2 sets of his books on
Architecture   2   2   0

May 16
Domat on the Civil Law in 2 vol. by Dr.
Straughan   2   5   0

May 31
The Institutes of the Laws of Engl(an)d by
Wood, Price   1   2   0

June 29
For 2 Books of Gardning of Langley's   ...   1   0   0

Aug. 16
Les Memoires de Madame de Monpensier   10   6

1729   May 12
To Sam(ue)l Buckley in part of a subscription for 7 vol. of Thuanus in Latin, for
w(hi)ch I have his receipt   4   4   0

May 20
Pd. to Hawkins, a Bookseller, for the 4th
volume of Père Catroux's Roman History,
translated by Bundi, w(hi)ch is to come
out in Aug(u)st next   1   3   6

1730   Feb. 4
To a Bookseller for Campbell's Vetruvius
Brittanicus, 3 vol, on Architecture, bound
in Blew-Paper   3   13   6

May 9
To Mr. Leoni, for 2 of his 2(n)d Volumes of
Architecture, by subscription   2   2   0

		£	s.	d.
1730	Oct. 20			
	To Monsr. Prevoreaux for 2 French Novels *p*(*ar*) Le Comte de Hamilton, and 2 books, Memoirs de Forbin	1	2	0
	Oct. 16			
	Pd. Mr. Prevoreaux, Bookseller, for 5 vols of Duo(*decimo*) of memoires pour L'histoire Du Cardinell de Richeleiu, and 2 other vols.	1	1	0
	Dec. 16			
	Pd. Jackson the Book-binder's bill ...	9	5	6
1731	May 4			
	Subscribed to a book of Agriculture by Mr. Trull (*sic*)		10	6
	May 13			
	To Monsr. Chaumette tow(*ar*)ds a subscription to his book of inventions	1	1	0
	May 20			
	To Mr. Leoni for Two Large Volumes of Paladio's Architecture, publish'd by Mr. Leoni	4	4	0
1732	Feb. 21			
	To Mr. Cole for a subscription, one Guinea, Pd. down for a book of letters he is to publish, Jan(*ua*)ry 1732	1	1	0
	Mar. 20			
	To Mr. James Leoni for 2 Volumes of Palladio in Large paper publish'd by himself ... ... (*not entered*)			
	Mar. 21			
	To Count Degenfeldt for a subscription to the History of Scotland in 2 Vol., of w(*hi*)ch one is already come out w(*hi*)ch is deliver'd to me w(*i*)th the Rect.	1	11	6
	Apr. 14			
	To Mr. Leoni for his Two Palladio's in Large paper, w(*hi*)ch I gave to Dr. Hollins	4	4	0

		£	s.	d.
Aug. 8				
Pd. Mr. N. Tindall for the first part of the subscription mony for his translation of Rapin's history of England. N.B. no receipt		1	1	0
Aug. 12				
To Mr. Innis, Bookseller, for Chambers's Dictionary, English, 2 vol.		7	7	0

1733 Jan. 8

Pd. Jackson, Book-binder, his bill in full	1	17	6

Feb. 6

Pd. the 2(n)d paym(en)t of a subscription Mr. Coles' Memoires of State affairs ...	1	1	0

Mar. 12

Pd. Count Degenfeldt to a subscription he pd. for me for Prince Cantimir's book, now translating by D. Wilkins and is to come out next Christmas	1	11	6

Mar. 16

To Dr. Mortimer for a first paym(en)t for a subscription of Kempser's book of Japan, w(hi)ch he is translating out of Dutch ...	2	2	0

Apr. 19

Pd. Jackson, the book-binder, for Miller the Gardener's Dictionary, £1 10s., and for a Pamphlet	1	11	0

Nov. 3

Pd. the subscription for the first payment for 2(n)d vol. of Bishop Burnet's History of his own time, at Mr. Innis's, Large paper		12	6

1734 Feb. 26

To Innis and Manby, Booksellers in Paul's Church-yard, for 2(n)d Part of Bishop Burnet's History of his own time, on large paper; by subscript(io)n £2 10s.			
For Sale's Alcoran, Just publish'd, 18s., in all and in full	3	8	0

Apr. 11

To Mr. Collins, the Author, for a book of the Presidents of claims of Baronies and the decisions thereon	1	5	0

		£	s.	d.

May 10
   Pd. Mr. Vaillant, French-Bookseller, for 4 vol in Duodecimo of the conquête des Portugais dans les Indes, and in full ...   14 0

May 18
   Pd. Parker, Bookseller, for the Builder's dictionary in 2 parts 12 0

June 15
   Pd. Monsr. Dunoyer, Bookseller for 3 vol of the Revolutions d'Espagne in 4to, and in full 1 10 0

July 30
   Pd. Monsr. De Noyer for French books ...   12 0

Aug. 26
   To Mr. Nicolas Tindal for the 2(n)d vol of Rapin's history of England, translated by himself, w(hi)ch is in full for that subscription, having pd. him a guinea before for the 1st 1 1 0
   N.B. Sd. Tindall is now school-Master at Chelmsford

Nov. 1
   Pd. Mr. Green, the bookseller at Chelmsford, for Melville's Memoires, & in full   8 0

1735 Jan. 3
   Pd. Jackson, Book-binder and bookseller, his bill in full 5 17 0

Feb. 24
   To a first subscription for Mr. Whiston's Josephus in English.
   N.B., he is to begin this book in March next 10 6

June 8
   To my Lady Sundon for a subscription for Stephen Ducks Poetry, w(hi)ch is to come out in April next 1 1 0

1736 Feb. 6
   To Jackson the bookseller for 4 volumes in Quarto of the present Peerage of England   1 5 0

		£	s.	d.

1736 Dec. 14

Pd. Mr. Tonson, Jun(*io*)r, a bill due for books to his father, a bookseller lately deceas'd, and in full **16 2 6**

Dec. 24

Pd. Monsr. Dunoyer, bookseller, his bill in full for 3 vols de l'etat de la France par Monsr. le Comte Boulainvilliers, £2 15s., and for 5 vol the Voyage de l'Afrique par Monsr. La Batt, 17s. 6d. **3 12 6**

1737 Feb. 9

Pd. Mr. Popple for a Long-book of maps with a red-Leather binding he bo(*ugh*)t for me **1 1 0**

Apr. 22

Pd. the subscript(*io*)n mony for the fourth volume of Pere Catroux and Rouille's Roman History **1 1 0**

May 28

To Mr. Clehand (?) a subscription on receiving from him a Custom-house book of Wine-Tables, calculated **16 0**

Sept. 6

Pd. Monsr. Denoyer, bookseller, for the Dictionaire de Com(*m*)erce in 3 vol., and in full **4 10 0**

Oct. 9

Bo(*ugh*)t of my Lady Ancram the Theatre de Grec, in 3 vol, Quarto **1 6 0**

Nov. 1

Pd. Mr. Alured Popple, secretary to the Board of Trade, for the Abridgemt. of the statutes he got for me **2 9 0**

Nov. 4

Bo(*ugh*)t at Innis's in Paul's Church-yard an acco(*un*)t of the Empire of Russia, w(*i*)th a map of Russia, writ by a Sweedish Offic(*e*)r who had been a prison(*e*)r there. Cost **15 0**

	£	s.	d.

1738 Jan. 11
Pd. Jackson, Bookseller, his bill in full ... 4 15 6

Feb. 25
Pd. Mr. Haines, £2 2s. w(*hi*)ch he had paid Mr. Forbes for a subscription Rec(*eip*)t for 2 Vol. of letters he is ab(*ou*)t to publish of the reign of Q. Eliz., one vol of w(*hi*)ch is to come out in one month ... 2 2 0

Mar. 27
Pd. Jackson. Bookseller, for a Treatise of the Law of nature, a Thick Quarto, cost 14 0

Apr. 18
Pd. Mr. Knapton, Bookseller, for 16 Heads, the Prints of great men, 17s., and for the case they are put in, 6s., in all ... ... (*not entered*)

Apr. 21
Pd. to the assignees in Com(*missi*)on of Bankrupt (*sic*) taken out agst. Mr. Prevost, Bookseller, 17 vol of Le Vassers History of Lewis 14th, and for the 8 Contes Mogul, and for La Mille & une nuite, 6 vol, 12(*m*)o, in full 3 18 6

July 29
Pd. Mr. Green, Book-seller at Chelmsford, for Dr Shaw's Account of Algires &ca, in folio and in full, one Vol 1 11 6

1739 Jan. 8
Pd. R. Chandler, Bookseller, by the hands of Mr. N. Tindall, for a set of the Magna Britannia in six vol, and in full 3 3 0

Apr. 12
Pd. to my Lady Bateman for a subscription for Middleton's Life of Cicero, and took a receipt of her 1 1 0

Sept. 27
Pd. for the Life of Phillip 2(*n*)d of Spain in 6 vol. Duodecimo 18 0

		£	s.	d.
1740	Jan. 15			
	Pd. Mr. Leoni 3 G(*uinea*)s in part of a sub-scription of 9 for 3 sets of his Treatise of Architecture, w(*hi*)ch is to come out at Christmas, 1740	3	3	0
	Jan. 16			
	Pd. Mr. Knapton for Chambers's Dictionary in 2 vol, 2d Edition, £4, and for Columna Rostrata, 14s. 6d., and in full of all ac-co(*un*)ts	4	14	6
	Feb. 18			
	Pd. for Temple Stanyon's first vol, octavo, of the original of the Grecians		5	0
	May 27			
	Subscrib'd to and paid as *p*(*er*) receipt to Mr. Thos. Cooke, Clergy-man, for the Copper Plates for his Translation of Plautus's Comedies	5	5	0
1741	Jan. 6			
	Pd. Jackson, Bookseller, his bill in full ...	1	9	0
	Mar. 10			
	Gave my Ld. Carteret by way of subscrip-tion for a book of Mr. (?) Metains, for w(*hi*)ch, I had no receipt, and desir'd my Ld. to write down my name in his List, and wou'd not write it my self	1	1	0
	Jan. 19			
	Pd. Mr. Jackson for Cary's Abridgem(en)t of the statutes in 2 vol. in folio, and in full...	2	5	0
	May 22			
	Pd. Mr. Jackson, book-binder, his bill in full	1	6	6
	Sept. 18			
	Pd. Jackson, Bookseller, his bill in full ...		17	0
1742	Jan. 12			
	Pd. — Jackson, Bookseller, his bill in full...		19	0
	Apr. 22			
	Pd. W(*illia*)m Spurret for fifteen volumes of Montfaucon's Antiquities, and in full of all accounts	13	13	0

		£	s.	d.
	Nov. 19			
	Pd. the Earl of Holdernesse for 2 vol. of Mr. Jervis Translation of Don Quixot in Quarto	1	10	0
1743	Jan. 31			
	Pd. Mr. Jackson, Book-seller, his bill in full	2	0	0
	Mar. 15			
	Pd. Mr. Jackson, Bookseller, for S(i)r William Temple's works in 2 folios, £1 10s., and for the History of the Bucaniers in America in 2 vol. Duod(ec)imo 6s., and in full	1	16	0
	Mar. 31			
	Bot. off and Pd. Monsr. Vaillant 2 vol. being the memoires of the Duke of Orleans, Regent de France		7	0
	Dec. 13			
	Pd. Mr. Knapton for Ainsworth's Dictionary		16	0
1744	Jan. 6			
	Pd. Dodsley, Bookseller, in full		14	0
	Jan. 14			
	To Mr. Jackson, my Book-seller, his bill in full	5	5	0
	Mar. 4			
	Pd. Mr. Collins in part of subscription of 2 Guineas for 8 vols, in octavo, of letters of the family of the Sidney's and Earls of Leicester	1	1	0
	Sept. 10			
	Pd. Mr. Jackson, Bookseller, in full ...	2	11	0
	Sept. 14			
	Monsr. Vailland pour L'Histoire de la Nouvelle France en 3 vol., 4(t)o, and in full	3	0	0
1746	Feb. 1			
	Pd. Jackson, Bookseller, his bill in full ...	1	2	6
	July 28			
	Pd. Mr. Arthur Collins for his 2 Vol. of the Sidney letters, bound	1	9	0

		£	s.	d.
1747	Feb. 23			
	Pd. Mr. Jackson, Book-seller, his bill in full	1	3	0
	Feb. 12			
	Pd. Dodsley for 2 sets of Roderick Random		12	0
1748	May 5			
	Pd. — Jackson, Book-binder, for six books Homer's Iliad in 3 volumes. Q(*uar*)to ...	1	4	0
	May 12			
	Pd. — Jackson, Book-binder, his bill in full	3	19	0
	Dec. 3			
	Pd. Monsr. Vaillant for Les Memoires de Sully, 8 vol., duod.	1	12	0
1749	Apr. 17			
	Pd. Mr. Wilson for Salmon's Chronology, 2 vol.		10	0
	Dec. 14			
	Pd. Dodsley for 2 books of S(*i*)r Thos. Edmondes state papers		12	0
1750	Jan. 6			
	Pd. Wilson, Book-seller, for 2 of Salmon's Geographic(*a*)l and Historical Gram(*m*)ar, and in full		19	0
	Jan. 18			
	Pd. Jackson, Book-seller, his bill in full ...	3	4	0
	Feb. 15			
	Pd. Mr. Tindall for a subscription for Postlethwaite's book ab(*ou*)t the Publique Revenues, £1 1s., more to be paid ...	1	1	0
	May 3			
	Pd. Mr. Nourse for Pausanius, &c, in French	1	10	0
	May 7			
	Pd. Mr. Wilson his bill in full for books and binding books	2	15	0
	Nov. 30			
	Pd. Dodisly for the Oeconomy of Human Life and for 4 of Steel's Plays bound, and in full		6	0

		£	s.	d.
1752	**Apr. 3**			
	Pd. Paul Vaillant for the memoires of Montgon.	1	4	0
	Apr. 6			
	Pd. Robert Wilson, Book-seller, his bill in full	2	19	0
	Apr. 25			
	Pd. Wilson, Book-seller, his bill in full ...	2	12	9
	July 29			
	Pd. Wilson for Hermes or the universal Gram(m)ar		6	0
	Nov. 22			
	Pd. Wilson, Book-seller, his bill in full ...		8	6
	Dec. 22			
	Pd. Mr. Tindall in full for 8 vols. of Spectators	1	10	0
	Pd. P. Vaillant for 2 Vols of Ovids Met. ...		8	0
1753	**Jan. 16**			
	Pd. — Dodsley for Le Siecle de Louis 14th, and in full		7	0
	Mar. 5			
	Pd. Jn. Jackson, Bookseller, his bill in full...		19	6
	Mar. 10			
	Pd. Paul Vaill(ant), Book-seller, his bill in full		8	0
	May 2			
	Pd. Js. Dodsley for Hanway's Travels, 3 vol.	1	10	0
	May 10			
	Pd. Mr. Tindal for Ludlow's memoires and other books	3	5	0
	June 21			
	Pd. — Jackson, Book seller, his bill in full...		12	0
1754	**Mar. 23**			
	Pd. Dodsley, Bookseller, in full		3	0
	Oct. 3			
	Bt. and pd. for 13 vols. of Rollins for my Lady Louisa	2	5	0

Pictures—transcript of all relevant entries
Original *spelling retained*

		£	s.	d.
1726	Oct. 12			
	To Mr. Jarvis for my Picture, a half length, in full	21	0	0
1727	Feb. 1			
	To an oval Picture of Mareshall Schonburg bought at an auction	1	2	0
1729	Feb. 10			
	To a Damag'd Picture of a Nun	1	15	0
	Apr. 11			
	To Mr. Waters, Frame-Maker, for a Gilt frame for a Head of the Mareschall Schonberg by Kneller w(*hi*)ch I bought at an auction	2	2	0
1730	May 13			
	Pd. Mr. Cox, the Auctioneer for a Picture bought at Sr. Godfrey Kneller's sale, of the Mareshall Duke Schonberg on Horseback, my wife's Grandfather, as by Cock's Rect. will appear	31	10	0
	May 21			
	To a German for Ring w(*i*)th Lady Caroline's Picture set in it	3	3	0
	July 17			
	Pd. Captain Smart's Daughter for a Picture of an old woman's head	3	3	0
1731	Mar. 6			
	To — Howard, Frame-maker, for a stretching-frame and Cleaning of the Picture of the Mareschall Duke of Schonbergh on Horse back, painted by S(*i*)r Godfrey Kneller for himself & bo(*ugh*)t by me at his auction, when his Pictures were sold	4	15	0
	June 26			
	To Mr. Amiconi, an Italian Painter, for a Picture of Architecture and little figures over the S.East Chimney below stairs in the principall Apartment	8	0	0

£ s. d.

N.B. there is also another of his drawing over the Drawing room Chimney peice, £12 12s., Pd. for at London.

July 21
Pd. Mr. Stranover, Fowl-piece Painter, in full for a Fowl-peice, wth. a Peacock in it at Large, ...   10 10 0

Oct. 12
To Mr. Howard, Frame-maker, his bill, the Mareschall Duke Schonburg's Picture &ca. 20 10 6

1732 Apr. 19
Pd. Mr. Gousset, Carver, in full for a Large frame of a Table and for Two frames for my wife's and my Picture at full Length, at Moulsham, ...   19 4 6

July 12
Pd. Mr. Enoch Seeman, Painter, in St. Martin's Lane for drawing my Picture at Length now at Moulsham Hall in Essex and in Robes, ...   21 0 0

1733 Sept. 4
For a Picture—a woman's head in a gold Frame, ...   2 2 0

1734 Jan. 30
To Mr. Wandermijn for my part towards Rafling for a Picture of Mr. Cole, ...   2 2 0

1735 Mar. 14
Pd. Rob(er)t Hunton for 12 Flower-prints painted, ...   1 5 0

Sept. 11
Pd. W(illia)m Waters, Frame-maker, in part of his bill given in of £28 7s. 0d., ...   15 15 0

1736 Apr. 9
To Mr. — Pine for Ten Prints taken from the Hangings in the house w(i)th. 11 Charts of the Sea-Coasts, and an acc(oun)t of the

Apr. 9—*cont.*

	£	s.	d.
several engagem(*en*)ts engrav'd in Copper to be deliver'd in 12 months, one paying one Guinea down, ...	1	1	0

1739 Feb. 2

Pd. Signor Soldi, an Italian Painter by the hands of Sign(*or*) Leoni for an Oval Picture of the Earl of Holdernesse to be put over one of the Doors in the dining-room in Moulsham Hall, ... 8 8 0

Feb. 14

Pd. Sign(*or*) Soldi by the hands of Mr. Leoni for an oval Picture drawn by him of the Earl of Ancram, and in full of all acco(*un*)ts, (*not entered—see below*)

Feb. 17

Pd. Sign(*o*)r Soldi for drawing an oval Picture of the Earl of Ancram, ... 8 8 0

Apr. 12

Pd. Martin at the Smyrna-Coffee-house for a picture of a horse of the Duke of Devonshire's call'd Childers, wth. a Rubbing-groom in blew, holding the horse by the bridle, and riding-Groom upon a Grey-crop'd horse, holding up one foot, cost 3 3 0

Apr. 20

The gilt frame, for the Pictures of Childers the running-horse, made by Mr. Waters and goes down into the Country to day, contains 17 foot, 9 inches of Frame-work and Gilding at 3s. 6d. p(*er*) foot, w(*hi*)ch am(*oun*)ts to £2 19s. 6d. besides the Packing case.

Oct. 10

Pd. Wm. Spurret for a Frame for a Picture of an old Lord Holdernesse, and in full... 2 12 6

		£	s.	d.

1740 May 6
Pd. for Bindin(*g*) one Large vol. the Prints
of the Hangings in the House of Lords of
the defeat of Spanish armada, 1588. By
(*blank*) Pine, ...   15   0

June 1
Pd. Mr. Slater, a painter, for doing the orna-
m(*en*)ts ab(*ou*)t 2 Pictures now at Moulsham, viz., that of the Earl of Holdernesse
and that of my Lord Ancram, and in
full, ...   2   2   0

Oct. 21
Pd. Mr. Gerrard Howard, Frame-maker, for
a frame for a Naked Picture of Beluchis,
now at Moulsham, £6, and for a Frame
for a Picture of Ulrick done by Vander-
myne, £3 3s., Box &ca, ...   10   1   0

1741 Mar. 12
Pd. Mr. Cox, Auctioneer, by the hands of
James West his Porter, for 3 Pictures bot.
at his auction, viz(*t*). for a man's Head by
Rembrandt, £5 5s., for the Birth of Pallas
by old Boulonge, an oval for a Ceiling,
£5 15s. 6d. For the sacrifice of Polyena by
La Herés, £4 4s., all sent down to Moul-
sham Hall   15   4   6

1742 Feb. 9
Pd. Monsr. Baudin for 2 Pictures done
after Marco Ricci. Extream Good Copies   7   7   0

Mar. 17
Pd. M(*r*). John Griffier for Cleaning a Picture of the Palatine family, done by Hon-
thurst and bought by me at Mrs. Howe's
auction, who was Daughter to Prince
Rupert, and in full, ...   4   4   0

March 18
Pd. Mr. Baudin a Painter for a Picture of
a Ruin by Marco Ricci, and in full,   ...   6   6   0

		£	s.	d.
March 20				
Pd. the Earl of Holdernesse for a Landscape he bought for me, drawn by Mr. Wotton, 15 Guineas $\frac{1}{2}$, ...		16	5	6
April 6				
Pd. Two Chairmen for carrying down to Moulsham Hall a Large Picture of the Palatine-family done by Honthurst, w(i)th a new frame, ...		1	1	0
May 6				
Pd. Mr. John Wootton for retouching, mending and improving a Landskip originally of his own painting, ...		10	10	0
N.B. it cost me at an auction, £16 5s., besides what I gave Mr. Wootton. There is in this picture a white horse a-feeding. I have sent it down this day to Moulsham Hall.				

1745 Sept. 7

		£	s.	d.
Pd. Mr. Baudin for 2 little Pictures by Vandervelt for Moulsham Hall, ...		2	2	0
Nov. 2				
Pd. Mr. James Leoni for a picture of Danae done by Berghem, and in full, ...		10	10	0

1747 June 20

		£	s.	d.
Pd. — Versovile for 2 Gilt frames for little Pictures, and in full, ...		1	16	0
Dec. 21				
Pd. Mr. Baudin for 2 pictures after Paulo Penini, ...		5	5	0

CHAPTER NINE

PUBLIC AFFAIRS

The value of Fitzwalter's accounts as source book material is enhanced by his comments, sometimes very direct and scathing, on those events which were uppermost in his mind. Most of them were written on those otherwise blank left hand pages (*see Intro-duction for the way in which the accounts were set out*), and they ranged from the movements of King George II to the fixing of new wheels on Fitzwalter's landau. Those on public affairs add very little to historical knowledge, but quite often they have a visual quality which gives them immediacy and considerable point.

His close connections with the Royal Family and the Court through his own Treasureship of the Household and his wife's kinship with George II is reflected in his comments. Over the years he recorded the King's eager departures to his beloved Hanover, *via* Harwich or Gravesend, and every reluctant return; the entry for May 13th, 1748, is a typical example: "This day the Parlia-ment was Prorogued to the 30th of June next, and about 4 this afternoon his Majesty set out for Graves-end in order to go to Holland on his way to Hanover; he set out w(*i*)th his usual impatience, tho' at that time not at all well." Fitzwalter was at Moulsham Hall on November 14th, 1737, when he received "an Alarm of the Queen's being dangerously ill" and immediately rushed to London. Six days later "she dy'd at 23 minutes past eleven at night; her Physitians mistook her distemper, thinking it was the gout".

Earlier, the Princess Royal's marriage to William, Prince of Orange, and her chance visit to Moulsham Hall are recorded by Fitzwalter; so, too, is a later visit by her sister, Princess Emily (*Amelia Sophia Eleanor*), although the full details would un-doubtedly have been given in that missing Moulsham Hall book. This is a pity: Fitzwalter's opinion of Princess Emily would have been worth reading even if it were more restrained than Lord Hervey's—"she was lively, false and a great liar; did many ill offices to people and no good ones, and for want of prudence said almost as many shocking things to their faces as for want of a good nature or truth she said disagreeable ones behind their backs". Later in life, she became a friend of Horace Walpole—a close union of sharp tongues.

The Princess's two brothers pass through the account books. That unpleasant young man, Frederick Prince of Wales, appears in only two entries: these refer to the 42½ guineas which Fitzwalter paid to Mrs. Sarah Taylor "for embroidering a Coat and Wastcoat w(i)th Gold on the marriage of the Prince of Wales w(i)th the Princesse of Saxe-Gotha, w(hi)ch was 27th of April last, 1736". There are several references, however, to William Augustus, Duke of Cumberland, the "Butcher" of Culloden, that "fleshy Cyclops", as Roger Fulford calls him. These arise from Fitzwalter's family pride: his stepdaughter's husband, the Earl of Ancram, served for a number of years in Cumberland's campaigns and was one of his aides-de-camp at the battle of Fontenoy. Fitzwalter's account of this hard-fought defeat (*see selective extracts*) is a neat piece of understatement.

The English armies were soon withdrawn to meet the Jacobite rising at home. Fitzwalter gives a running commentary on the Forty-Five, from Prestonpans and Falkirk to the siege of Stirling and the final defeat of Prince Charles Edward at Culloden, and adds the trial of Simon Fraser, Lord Lovat, as a postscript. Most of these entries have been fully given by R. S. Adams in Vol. 60 of the *Essex Review,* but Fitzwalter's highly partisan account of Culloden, written as soon as the news was brought to him, is so fresh and vivid that it deserves repetition in the selective extracts in this chapter, even if it causes apoplexy in Highland readers.

Fitzwalter made very few references to contemporary politics, but they are sufficient to show his firm support of Walpole and his contempt for Sir William Wyndham and Lord Carteret. This is seen clearly in the entries for November 1739 and February 1741 (see selective extracts). These refer to the war with Spain and France in which he was obviously deeply interested, and not solely because of Ancram's service under Cumberland. He records, for instance, Vernon's expeditions of 1739 and 1741 to the West Indies, and the capture of Marshal Belleisle in 1745.

His entries relating to his own public appointments (as Chief Commissioner of the Board of Trade and Plantations in 1735, as Lord Treasurer of the Household in 1737 and as Lord Lieutenant of Essex and Custos Rotulorum in 1741) are remarkable mainly for the multiplicity of fees which had to be paid! In 1735, the *official* fees were £60 10s., but there were also the consequent fees and tips: he even had to pay "Mr. Gillibrand for taking out a Privy-Seal to empower me to receive my salary". But he did not stay long at the Board; by 1737 he "was heartily tyr'd of it" and was delighted to become Treasurer of the Household, a post he retained until only a few weeks before his death.

References
Lord Hervey's devastating comment on the Princess Emily is given on pp. 44–45 of his *Memoirs*, edited by Romney Sedgwick (1963 edition).

Public Affairs—selective extracts
Original spelling retained

1732 June 3   £ *s.* *d.*

K. George 2(n)d went from St. James's down the River in order to pass over to Holland on his way to Hanover, but did not land at Helvost-Sluyce till Saturday June the 10th. From thence persu'd his Journey to Hannover w(i)th all Expedition when he arriv'd.

Sept. 14

Thursday the 14th of Sept(*embe*)r the King came from Hannover, arriv'd at Helvost-sluys the 16th, was detain'd there by Contrary winds till the 24th and arriv'd in the River of Thames and from thence at Kensington the 26th by 5 o'-clock in the evening, 1732.

1733 Nov. 13

Bot. of one De Fromantell 2 yds $\frac{1}{2}$ of a Rich Brocade of French stuff, on a Green Velvet ground for the Marriage of the Princesse Royal w(i)th the Prince of Orange 16 16 0

1734 Nov. 21 £ s. d.

The Princesse Royal having layn at Harwich 17 days for a wind for Holland, the King order'd her to wait no longer, but to come away directly from Dover, w(hi)ch she did and stopping at an Inn at Chelmsford, as soon as we had advise of it, my Lady Fitz-Walter took her Coach and imediately went to her to invite her to Moulsham, she found her at dinner, and rec(eive)d her in the kindest and most obliging manner in the world, and leaving her people to dine, step'd into my wife's Coach w(i)th her, and came up hither and staid here abt. an hour and a half and drunk Tea & Coffee, but wou'd have nothing else. I press'd her as much as was proper to stay and lye here, w(hi)ch she seem'd very desirous to have done, but she said as her Route was fix'd and the Guards laid by the King's order it was not in her power. She went that evening to Rumford and lay at an Inn there, next day went over London-Bridge and lay at Dartford in her way to Dover, but did not go to St. James nor saw none of the Royal Family as she went thro' London. She staid at Dover for a wind about a week and then went over in one of the King's Yachts to Calais, where the Prince of Orange her Husband met her, and after having recover'd the fatigues of her voyage (being farr gone w(i)th Child) in five or six days they set out by land for Holland.

1735 Jan. 23

being the day the King made his speech to the Houses and accepted Mr. Onslow for Speaker, I gave my Ld. Chancell(o)rs mes-

	£	s.	d.

Jan. 23—*cont.*

senger that bro(*ugh*)t me my writ of sumons for this new Parliam(*en*)t some time before   1   1   0

May 16

To the King's footmen on my being made first Lord (Com(*m*)ission(*e*)r of Trade and Plantations and sworn of the Privy-Counsil, Two Guineas. To the Queen's footmen the same. To the yeomen of the Guard the same   6   6   0

May 22

Pd. P. Sharp, Keeper of the Records, a Note of Fees due on my being sworn a privy-Counsillor   26   0   0

May 22

Pd. John Shore, Serg(*ean*)t-Trumpet, his Fee also on my being sworn a Privy-Counsillor   2   2   0

May 23

Took my seat at the Board at the Plantation-office as first Com(*m*)issioner, and the new-Com(*m*)ission so appointing me in the room of the Earl of Westmorland (re-mov'd) was this day open'd at the Board and read, and then pd. the usual Fees or Gratuities to Door-keepers &ca   3   3   0

June 3

Pd. Mr. Preverau of the Duke of Newcastle's office my share of the Expence for passing the Com(*m*)ission constituting me first Ld. Com(*missione*)r at the Head of the Board of Trade and Plantations and of Mr. Rich(ar)d Plumer one of the Com-(*missione*)rs. at the sd. Board, £60 10s. 0d., five Guineas of w(*hi*)ch was for his trouble. The whole was £120 15s. 0d. ...   60   10   0
(See D/DM O1/3 for original account.)

	£	s.	d.

June 4

To the Deputy Clerk of the Crown's Clerk for bringing a Dedimus to the Plantation office to empower Col(*one*)l Bladen to give me the oath of a Justice of the Peace w(hi)ch I took accordingly this day   ...   3 3 0

Oct. 15

Pd. Mr. Gillibrand for taking out a Privy-seal to empower me to receive my salary as first Com(*missione*)r at the Board of Trade £25 12s. 2d., for Treas(*u*)ry fees £2 15s. 3d.(?), Auditors' Fees £1 1s. 0d.(?) for entring the new Com(*missio*)n £1 1s. 0d., Letter of Attorny & entring it, 8s. 3d. & for other Fees 43 4 6

1736 Jan. 8

Pd. Mr. Sadler a Clerk in the Pell's office for entring my Com(*missio*)n there 1 1 0

Jan. 10

To the Marshal's-men 10 0

Jan. 10

To the yeomen of the Guard 1 1 0

Jan. 13

To the Messenger of the Counsil-office ...   10 6

Jan. 19

To S(*i*)r R.W.'s serv(*an*)ts 3 3 0

Jan. 19

To the King's footmen 1 1 0

Jan. 20

To the yeomen of the Guard 1 1 0

(*Subsequent New Year's entries of this kind, not extracted*)

Apr. 25

Gave my Lord Holdernesse at Moulsham for his Pocket at his coming to London to enquire what day the Prince of Wales to be married 3 3 0

	£	s.	d.

May 3

Pd. Mrs. Sarah Tailor for embroidering a Coat and Wastcoat w(*i*)th Gold on the marriage of the Prince of Wales w(*i*)th the Princesse of Saxe-Gotha, w(*hi*)ch was 27th of April last **44 12 0**

1737 **May 20**

I kiss'd the King's hand on being made Treasurer of the King's House-hold, and his Majesty in his closet deliver'd into my hand the White-staff, w(*hi*)ch my Ld. De La Warr resign'd that morning, on his being appointed Gov(*erno*)r of New-York, and the same day I gave up my Post of beiing first Lord Com(*missione*)r of the board of Trade and Plantations, w(*hi*)ch I enjoy'd 2 years and one month and was heartily tyr'd of it, and desir'd I might exchange it for something else or said I wou'd throw it up.

June 21

To the King's Watermen **1 1 0**

June 23

I was sworn into my office by the Duke of Dorset, then Lord Steward, at his house in Whitehall, and the 25th Pd. the Fees

May 28

To the Ringers at Chelmsford, being the first time I came down since my being Treasurer to his Majesty's House-hold   ...   **1 4 0**

July 30

I went to my lodgings at Hampton-Court w(*i*)th my Lady Fitz-Walter and carried the Earl of Holdernesse and the Countesse and Earl of Ancram w(*i*)th us, and staid to the 5th of Sept(*embe*)r following, in w(*hi*)ch time I spent as follows—

N.B. Spent at Hampton-Court during my stay there **160 18 0**

	£	s.	d.

Sept. 5
Spent at Richmond dining at the Castle Inn   2   10   0

Sept. 5
Gave away in seeing the Queen's Garden
at Richmond   12   6

Sept. 6
N.B. Pd. in Aug(*u*)st last at Hampton-
Court to Mr. Beal, secretary to the Duke
of Dorset, Ld. Steward of the Household, £10 10s. 0d., for a war(*ra*)nt to swear
me in as Treas(*ure*)r of the House-hold,
and for the stamps to sd. Warr(*an*)t
£6 0s. 0d. in all   16   10   0

N.B. Pd. in Aug(*u*)st last, at Hampton-Court,
the Fee due to my Ld. Chamberlain's
secretary, for my Warr(an)t for 1000
ounces of White Plate,

Nov. 14
Return'd to the Pall-mall w(*i*)th my Lady
Fitz-Walter leaving the Earl of Holder-
nesse and the Earl and Countesse of
Ancram at my house in Essex, on an
Alarum of the Queen's being in Extream
danger of Life. Spent at Rumford   (*not entered*)

N.B. The Queen was taken ill Nov(*embe*)r
(*blank*) being a Wednesday. She dy'd
Nov(*embe*)r 20th at 23 minutes past
eleven at night, her Physitians mistook
her distemper, thinking it was Gout. And
was buried the 17th of Dec(*embe*)r following

Nov. 20
Pd. for four Quire of Black edg'd paper and
3 sticks wax   7   0

Dec. 14
Remove this day to London w(*i*)th my whole
family in order to Walk at the Funeral of
the late Queen, w(*hi*)ch is to be on Saturday, 17th Ins(*tan*)t.

1738 May 27   **£ s. d.**
      To Mrs Dupuis, Milliner, her bill in full for
          things had of her for the Countesse of
          Ancram when she held up the Princesse-
          Royals Train at her Marriage w(*i*)th the
          Prince of Orange, and in full 50 0 0

      Dec. 23
      Gave Mr. Skinner, one of the under Clerks
          of the Green-Cloth for receiving four
          Quarters, the salary due to me at Trea-
          surer of his Majesties House-hold, *viz*.,
          £1 1s. 0d. p(*e*)r Q(*uarte*)r 4 4 0

1739 Aug.
      In Aug(*us*)t, Admiral Vernon sail'd w(*i*)th a
          squadron of the King's ships into the West
          Indies, winter'd at Jamaica and, Feb-
          (*rua*)ry, took Porto-bello, and some time
          after he took Fort Chagres also from the
          Spaniards.

      Oct. 26th, 1740 S(*i*)r Chaloner Ogle sail'd
          w(*i*)th 25 ships of the Line to Joyn Vernon
          in the West Indies, and had under his
          Convoy Transports w(*i*)th 7000 Marines
          on Board w(*hi*)ch were to be Joyn'd in the
          West Indies by 5 or 6000 men rais'd there
          in order to Attack Carthagena.

      N.B.   There were Two squadrons of French
          and another Spanish men of Warr
          amounting to 32 or 33 ships sail'd for
          those seas ab(*ou*)t one month before ours,
          wch. had been kept in the River near
          three months by Contrary winds.

      Sept. 26
      Pd. Mr. Sidwick his and the House-keeper's
          Fees at the Jewel-office for the 1000
          ounces of silver-plate allow'd me by the
          King as Treas(*ure*)r of his House-hold ...   4 9 0

Nov. 23   £ *s.* *d.*

An Address by both Houses of Parliam(*en*)t was made to the King, the speaker of both Houses walking up a-breast, the Address read by my Lord Chancell(*o*)r Hardwicke, Mr. Onslow, Speaker of the House of Comons standing equal w(*i*)th him. The address was a resolution of the house of Comons to w(*hi*)ch the Lords agreed, that the King be advised or desir'd not to make peace w(*i*)th the Crown of Spain, till a preliminary shou'd be settl'd and agreed upon, that the English shou'd have a free and uninterrupt(*e*)d navigation to and from our American Colonies w(*i*)thout being liable to be stopp'd search'd or visited on any pretence whatever.

N.B. This Ridiculous motion was made by S(*i*)r W(*illia*)m Windham, ab(*ou*)t six weeks after warr was declar'd w(*i*)th Spain, it being at that time very extraordinary to talk of an Article of peace when the war was hardly begun, but this silly motion was by him (then in the opposition) in hopes Walpole (then first minister) wou'd oppose it, but in this Windham and his party were bit, and the address went.

1740 May 13, 14

When I was at Gravesend to attend his Majesty on Board his yacht before he set sail for Holland, I spent (my Lord Holdernesse and my Lord Ancram being w(*i*)th me) the sum of 6 10 0

May 24

The Earl of Holdernesse went from my House to Dover, went o'Board Sunday 25th and Landed at Boulogne in 4 hours and ½ w(*i*)th an intention to proceed on directly to Brussels and from thence to

May 24—*cont.*   £   *s.*   *d.*
Cassel in order to be at the Marriage of
our Princesse Mary w(*i*)th Prince
Frederick the son of Prince William of
Hesse-Cassel. N.B. She was espous'd
there the 8th last by Proxy, and kept ever
since by Contrary winds, till the (*blank*).
The Proxy was her own Brother the Duke
of Cumberland.

June 6
The Wind coming ab(*ou*)t fair the Princesse
of Hesse went aboard this morning in
order to Land at Rotterdam, and so
persue her Journey to Cassel to her young
Husband.

N.B. It was yesterday four weeks since she
was married.

1741   Jan. 23
A sloop arriv'd here w(*i*)th letters from
Admiral Vernon at Jamaica. She sail'd
from thence the 13th of Dec(*embe*)r; they
then had no news of S(*i*)r Chaloner Ogle's
squadron w(*hi*)ch we here judge must
have been at Jamaica by the 25th of
Dec(*embe*)r last. These letters bring advice
that Col(*one*)l Blakeney w(*i*)th 3500 men
rais'd on the American Continent were
safely arriv'd at Jamaica, and waited the
arrival of my Lord Cathcart's forces in
order to Joyn them to go upon the intended Expedition. When this sloop came
away there were 20 French men of warr
at Hispaniola, w(*hi*)ch is w(*i*)thin 2 days
sail of Jamaica, and the people of Jamaica
not a little uneasie at their Neighbour-
hood, Admiral Vernon not having w(*i*)th
him at that time above 10 or 11 Line-
o'-Battle-ships, tho' in expectation every

Jan. 23—*cont.*   £   s.   d.
day of being joyn'd by Ogle's squadron,
w(hi)ch consists of 20 ships of the line.
The Spaniards have at the same time, 14
ships of the Line at Carthagena.

Feb. 13
Friday, Feb(*rua*)ry 13th, 1740/41, the same
motion was made in both Houses of Par-
liam(*en*)t, in the House of Lords by my
Lord Carteret and in the House of
Comons by Mr. Sands, viz., that an
Humble Address be presented to his
Majesty that he will remove the Right
Hon(*ourab*)all Walpole, &ca, &ca, from
his presence and Counsils for ever. And
this address was propos'd to go to the
King, simple and plain and unsupported
w(*i*)th any reasons to be laid before his
Majesty. My Lord spoke Two hours by
way of his motion, and as long speeches
beget long speeches the House of Lords
sat till one o'Clock in the morning. Those
for the address made a very bad figure in
this day's debate, having made so unwar-
rantable, so unjustifiable, so unpresidented
and so unparliamentary a motion, and
upon the division there appear'd

       for the Question   47
       Ag(*ain*)st it   89
                      —
       Majority   42

May 7
May 7th, 1741, the King having this day
made a short declaration to his Counsil of
his intentions to go over to his German
dominions in order to endeav(*ou*)r to settle
the present disorder in Germany, and that
he should leave the Care of these Kingdoms in the same hands he did last year,

May 7—*cont.*   £   *s.   d.*

we th(*e*)n kiss'd his Majesty's hand in the
Counsil Chamber and he set out between
4 and 5 o'Clock, and went in his Barge to
Gravesend and so on Board the Carolina
yacht.

1742 May 25

N.B. This day the bill of Indemnication
for all the Rogues and (*blank*) in the three
Kingdoms to come in and give evidence
ag(*ain*)st the Earl of Orford was rejected
in the House of Lords by 92 Ag(*ain*)st 47,
on the Question whether it be comitted or
not.

June 3

Gave Mr. White one of the Clerks in the
House of Lords for making the new
alterations in my book of the standing
orders of the House of Lords   1   1   0

1743 Apr. 27

The King went from St. James's between
four and five o'Clock in the morning for
Graves-end and Landed at Helvost-Sluys
May 2(*n*)d abt. six in the evening. The
Earl of Holdernesse set sail in the Pacquet
frrom Harwich May 1st and Landed
Helvost 5 hours before the King. My Lord
goes directly to the army encamp'd in the
Plains of Frankfort and waits there as a
Lord of his Bed-Chamber till his Majesty
comes, who makes some stay at Hannover
first. The Duke went over w(*i*)th the King
who after having stay'd Two days at the
Hague follow'd the King to Hannover.

Nov. 15

Came this day to London w(*i*)th my family
to meet the King who came also this day
to St. James's from Hannover where (*he*)

Nov. 15—*cont.*   £   *s.*   *d.*

had been ever (*since*) he left the army
upon the Rhine and when the Princesse
Louisa had been married by Proxy to the
Prince Royal of Denmark.

1744   July 31

The Earl and Countesses of Holdernesse
went on board the Mary yacht in order to
proceed to the Hague and from thence to
Vienna and from thence to Venise, to
w(*hi*)ch place his Majesty has sent him
as Embassad(*o*)r-Extraordinary.

1745   Feb. 18

Maraschal Belleille and his Brother having
been taken prisoners in passing over part
of the Hanover dominions were this day
carry'd to the Keep at Windsor, where
they were put under the care of Major-
Gener(*a*)ll. Folliot and 8 Capt(*ain*)s of his
Majestie's Guard, and Tables Kept for
them at King's Expence. Whither this is
wisely or sillyly done a little time will
show.

Apr. 5

The Duke set out for Harwich in order to go
to the Hague and from thence to Brussels
in order to take upon himself the Comand
of the allied army then approaching Cam-
paigne, and on the Saturday the 6th, my
Lord Ancram being one of his aides-de-
Camp set out for Dover and from thence
to Ostend in order to Joyne the Duke
as soon as possible at Brussells.

Apr. 30

The Confederate army under the Comand
of the Duke of Cumberland attack'd the
French army in their intre(*n*)chm(*en*)ts).
Fronted and Flank'd both in the right and
left w(*i*)th Cannon, the French then be-

Apr. 30—*cont.*   £   *s.*   *d.*

seiging Tournay, w(*i*)th more than 80,000 men, w(*i*)th an army of about 45,000 men we attack'd them for 8 hours and a half. We were at last oblig'd to retreat, the enemy not daring to persue us, or molest our retreat.

Sept. 25

Return'd this day to London w(*i*)th my lady Fitz-Walter and Mr. Warrender on the news of the King's forces under the Comand of S(*i*)r John Cope being defeated by the Highlanders in Scotland. Spent on the Road   7   0

Oct. 16

Came up to Town this day w(*i*)th my family in order to the meeting of the Parliam(*en*)t w(*hi*)ch is to be tomorrorw. Spent on the Road   7   0

Nov. 16

My Lord Ancram march'd from Windsor at the Head of my Lord Mark Kerr's Regim(*en*)t of Dragoons, Nov(*embe*)r 16th, 1745, in order to Joyn the army w(*hi*)ch was to assemble in or near Lancashire under the Comand of the Duke in order to oppose the Rebels.

1746   Jan. 17

My Lord Ancram return'd to London, having undergon vast fatigues and suffer'd much from the severities of the season, yet held out extreamly well till after the attack upon the Rebels at Clifton where he acted as Brigad(*ie*)r-Gener(*a*)l, and comanded on that occasion all the Horse and Dragoons.

Jan. 25

General Hawley having met w(*i*)th some disgrace from the Rebels, the Duke in order to take the Comand of the army

Jan. 25—*cont.*   £ *s. d.*

upon him, set out from St. James's on Saturday at one o'Clock in the morning, Jan(*ua*)ry 25th, and got to Edinburg on Thursday, 30th, at 3 o'Clock in the morning. And on Friday morning being the 31st he march'd the army to Attack the Rebells who were then besieging Stirling Castle where Gen(*e*)r(*a*)l Blakney comanded and made a Gallant defence. But upon the Duke w(i)th the King's Troops consisting of about 6,000 men (*? attacking*), a Panick struck the Rebels and made a most precipitate flight and broke and divided themselves into several small bodies; some went to Montrose in order to get off by sea and the Pretender's son went to the West w(*i*)th some of the Clans, as is suppos'd to go on Board from the Isle of Mull, where he landed first about the end of July last, 1745, w(*i*)th seven persons w(*i*)th him. The Duke is now persuing of them.

Feb. 9

My Lord Ancram set out from London for Edinburgh w(*i*)th my Lord Mark Kerr, Jan(*ua*)ry, Sunday the 26th and arriv'd there on Saturday, Feb(*rua*)ry 9th, and went next day to Perth to Joyn. At Stirling, Perth and Montrose we took all all (*sic*) the Canon belonging to the Rebels w(*hi*)ch they left behind them in their precipitate flight more North Wards. The Duke is march'd to Aberdeen.

Apr. 16

April 16th, 1746, The Duke attack'd near Culloden house, w(*hi*)ch is a small distance from Invernesse. The Rebels were upwards of 8000 men. The King's army not exceeding 7000. The Rebels made a

April 16th 1746 — The Duke attack'd near Culloden house in
wch was a small distance from Inverness. The Rebels were upwards
of — 8000 men. The King's army not exceeding — 7000 — The Rebels
made a furious attack on one wing of the King's army, but that not —
succeeding they immediately turn'd their backs and fled with the utmost
precipitation — of them there was kill'd and taken prisoners good —
many — our King's side not one hundred men kill'd — But my Lord Robert Kerr
Brother to my Lord Ancram was there kill'd gallantly for the
King and in defence of the laws and liberties of his country
So fell the handsomest and the finest young fellow in Great Britain
by the hands of those execrable villains — They say my Lord Ancram —
kill'd four of the Rebels with his own hand, and had his sword broke then —
& my Lord Seidmourade who fell down on his knees and beg'd his life —
who took him prisoner.

FITZWALTER'S ACCOUNT OF THE BATTLE OF CULLODEN

Apr. 16—*cont.*   £   *s.*   *d.*

furious attack on one wing of the King's
army, but that not succeeding they immediately turn'd their Backs and fled w(*i*)th
the utmost precipitation. Of them there
was kill'd and taken prisoners ab(*ou*)t
4000, on the King's side not one Hundred
men kill'd. But my Lord Robert Kerr
Brother to my Lord Ancram was there
kill'd Gallantly for the King and in defence of the Laws and Liberties of his
Country. So fell the handsomest and the
finest young fellow in Great-Britain by
the hands of the Execrable villains. The
same day my Lord Ancram kill'd four of
the Rebels w(*i*)th his own hand, and had
his Pistol at the head of my Lord Kil-
marnock who fell down on his knees and
begg'd his Life—so he took him prisoner.

Oct. 23

Octob(*e*)r 23(*r*)d, 1746, the Earl and Countesse of Holdernesse landed in England
from his Embassy at Venice, after having
been absent from home ever since the first
day of Aug(*u*)st, 1744. My Lord Darcy
was born at Venice, Sept(*embe*)r 6th,
1745, Christn'd George, the King being his
Godfather.

1747 Feb. 24

The Earl of Ancram being the first Lord of
the Bed-Chamber to his R.H. the Duke set
out from London Tuesday Feb(*rua*)ry
24th, 1746, in order to follow him to the
Hague where the Duke had been about 3
weeks before. My Lord waited at Harwich
8 days for a wind.

Mar.

Simon Fraser Lord Lovat being empeach'd
of High Treason by the Comons for being
deeply concern'd in the late Rebellion, his
Tryal before the House of Peers began in
Westminster-Hall on Monday, March 9th,
1746, and ended the 19th, and was found

Mar.—*cont.*   £   *s.   d.*

Guilty, *Nemine contradicente*, by 117
Lords then present. My Lord Hardwicke,
Lord High-Chancell(*o*)r of Great Britain
being then for the 2(*n*)d time appointed
Lord High Steward.

N.B. Three days out of the Ten, the House
did not sit, so that the Tryal lasted but
seven days.

1748   Feb. 13

The King put the seals of Secretary of State
into the hands of the Duke of Bedford,
the Earl of Chesterfield having resign'd
them the Saturday sennet before.

Feb. 24

The Duke set out from St. James's at half
an hour past three in the morning for
Harwich in order to go on Board the
yacht there for Holland, the Weather
being extream sharp w(*i*)th a severe Frost
and much snow.

Mar. 22

The Earl of Ancram set out from London
to Joyn the Duke at the Hague, who
Comands the army in Flanders this year.
My Lady Ancram went w(*i*)th my Lord
and my Lady Aylesbury w(*i*)th Collnl.
Conway. They all went from Greenwich
on a yacht together.

Apr.

Preliminaries for a General peace were
signed at Aaix La Chapelle April 19th
1748, by the Ministers of England,
France and the States-General, and all
hostilities by land ceas'd in a few days,
and by sea, in different parts of the world
according to the usual stipulated points
of time in the like cases.

May 13

This day the Parliament was Prorogued to
the 30th of June next . . . and about 4 this

£ s. d.

May 13—*cont.*

afternoon his Majesty set out for Gravesend in order to go to Holland on his way
to Hannover, he set out w(*i*)th his usual
impatience, tho' at that time not all well.

July 13

Came to London w(*i*)th my Lady Fitz-
Walter, to return Princesse Emilie thanks
for the Honour of her visit and dining
w(*i*)th my Lady Fitz-Walter this sumer at
at Moulsham Hall.

1749 May 24

The Earl of Holdernesse set out w(*i*)th my
Lady from Moulsham-Hall to Harwich in
his way for Holland to w(*hi*)ch place he is
sent to reside as Minister Plenip[*o*]tentiary
from the K. of England to the States
General.

1750 Nov. 4

The King return'd from Hannover and
landed at Harwich ab(*ou*)t 12 o'Clock at
Noon on Sunday, Nov(*embe*)r 4th, 1750,
and arriv'd at St. James's ab(*ou*)t half an
hour after Ten that night, a passage of 20
hours and fine Calm weather. The Birth-
day was kept Nov(*embe*)r 14th.

1751 Apr. 28

The Earl of Holdernesse then Minister
Plenipotentiare to the States-Generall had
leave to come over and Landed in
England this day and Lay at Moulsham-
Hall the same night. I went in June following to Moulsham. He came down to
me there, in 3 or 4 days, and return'd to
London Monday 17th of sd. Ins(*tan*)t
June and on Tuesday, 18th of sd. Ins(*tan*)t
the Duke of Bedford Secretary of State
for the Southern Province resig'd (*sic*) the
seals w(*hi*)ch the King Imediately Gave
into the hands of the Earl of Holdernesse.

Apr. 28—*cont*   £   *s.   d.*

Ab(*ou*)t the same time the Earl of Gran-
ville was made Presid(*en*)t of the Counsill,
My Lord Hartington (eldest son of the
D. of Devonshire) was made Master of
the Horse, th(*e*) Earl of Sandwich
remov'd and My Lord Anson in his stead
put at the Head of the Board of Ad-
miralty.

N.B.   This is the first day of the new-style
in England.

1752   Feb. 8

The King sing'd (*sic*) my Lord Ancram's
Comiss(*io*)n to be Collon(*e*)ll of my Lord
Mark Kerr's Regiment of Dragoons.

THE END

INDEX

Personal and place names which appear only incidentally in the account books have not been included in this Index. The names of some craftsmen and tradesmen have been omitted, but page references to their work can be found under *Occupations*.

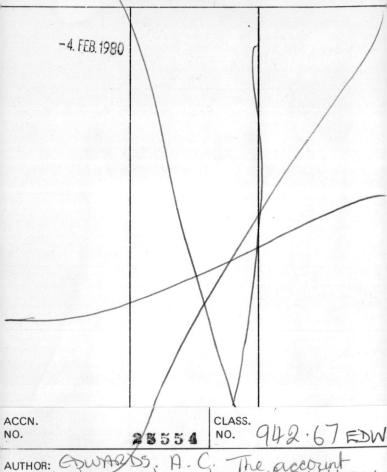